A Spirit-Baptized People

LIVING WHAT WE BELIEVE
Volume 4

A Spirit-Baptized People

With Leader's Guide for SMALL GROUPS by J. Ben Wiles

French L. Arrington

ISBN: 978-1-940682-58-7

CONTENTS

FOREWORD

Why Living What We Believe?

Why indeed? The Living What We Believe six-volume series of small group/class studies is written and specifically developed for the purpose of making Pentecostal disciples of Jesus Christ. For those seeking to know more about living the Christ-life, there is plenty here to be learned and discussed. However, Living What We Believe (all six volumes) has much more to offer than biblical knowledge and doctrine alone. This series has been especially created to foster relational discipleship within a community of believers for the purpose of transformational life-change! Making disciples is all about developing true followers of Jesus Christ while understanding that the person and work of the Holy Spirit himself is intimately and undeniably involved in this lifelong process. It is the Holy Spirit who helps disciples become more like Jesus.

The Living What We Believe six-volume series is a complete 24-week discipleship study (though a participant or group is free to use any one volume alone, or in any order they prefer). This series both understands and is built upon the truth that only disciples make other disciples! Coming together as the body of Christ within the context of a small group is an essential and fruitful means by which Jesus' Great Commission (Matthew 28:18-20), can be fulfilled. Likewise, coming together as the body of Christ within the context of a small group is also a natural and organic means by which Jesus' Great Commandment (Matthew 22:36-40) can find a more productive fulfillment.

Over the course of the six volumes of this series, the reader/participant will be provided both biblical/ doctrinal teaching based on the fourteen points of the Church of God Declaration of Faith as well as the opportunity to reflect upon and discuss the practical ramifications of living out what we believe . . . all within the relational context of small group discipleship. The general framework of the series is based upon, and generally guided by an understanding of the "Fivefold Gospel" (i.e. Jesus is our Savior, Jesus is our Sanctifier, Jesus is our Spirit-Baptizer, Jesus is our Healer, and Jesus is our coming King).

The format of the Living What We Believe series is simple, relational and structured specifically to make true disciples, as well as assisting disciple-makers to fulfill their mission. Each of the six volumes, (*A Believing People, A Saved People, A Sanctified People, A Spirit-Baptized People, A Healed People, An Expectant People*) is a four-week study with each week divided into five days. Each participant reads, reflects, and reacts to each of these days at home in his or her personal time. Each day will feature several components which enable the growth process of the disciple at a personal level:

- Search the Scripture (selected Scripture readings).
- Answer the Following Questions (reflective questions directly relevant to the Scripture selection).
- Yield to the Spirit—divided into three sub-sections:
  1. "Know"—relating to one's intellect (your mind).
  2. "Be"—relating to one's passion (your heart).
  3. "Do"—relating to one's behavior (your hands).
- Offer a Prayer—the conclusion of each day.

After the five daily personal interactions, the participant will join with the other members (who have likewise personally worked through the sessions) for the weekly small group session. Led by the leader/facilitator, the weekly small group meetings provide members with the time to open up, give responses, and yield to the corporate and personal leading of the Holy Spirit. The leader/facilitator does not decide the response from members, but rather asks questions and helps guide group members to the practical, behavioral outworking of what we believe as Pentecostal members of the body of Christ. Each group session is about sharing, relating, learning, and being aware of the presence of the Holy Spirit. There will be a key scripture for discussion in each group session. As you work through the studies, you will note information about the "Opening," "Prayer," "Testimony," "Discussion Questions," and the section we refer to as "Yielding to the Spirit." Group leaders will find much more very helpful information concerning both starting and leading a small group from series Assistant Editor J. Ben Wiles in the following sections of this volume. If you are a group leader/facilitator, always make sure to publicly welcome the presence of the Holy Spirit to guide, teach, convict, encourage, and unify all those who are present for the weekly group session. Remember that the ultimate benefit of the Living What We Believe discipleship series is not only the transmission of biblical/doctrinal teaching, but also it is the Spirit-led, life-transformation of men and women into healthy disciples of Jesus Christ!

As general editor and publishers of this disciple-making series, we wish to express our thanks and sincere appreciation to Assistant Editor J. Ben Wiles, whose *People of the Spirit* served as the primary template for Living What We Believe. We also wish to thank Lenae Simmons for her diligent labor in the copy editing, layout, and design of this work. Finally, we wish to convey our respect and gratitude to the scholars who authored the individual volumes:

Volume One—*A Believing People* by J. Ben Wiles

Volume Two—*A Saved People* by Lee Roy Martin

Volume Three—*A Sanctified People* by J. Ben Wiles

Volume Four—*A Spirit-Baptized People* by French L. Arrington

Volume Five—*A Healed People* by Daniel Tomberlin

Volume Six—*An Expectant People* by French L. Arrington

These authors and their insightful work and commitment to making disciples for Jesus Christ cannot be overstated.

Whether Pentecostal, evangelical, or any believer wishing to take up the cross and follow Jesus, we highly recommend all six volumes of the Living What We Believe series. If you are a disciple-maker, this series is at your service. While it can certainly be used for individual study, we highly recommend this small group experience.

O. Wayne Brewer, D.Min   Pamela R. Brewer, M.A.
Men's Discipleship   *Women's Discipleship*
Adult Discipleship Church of God International Offices

General Editors: O. Wayne and Pamela R. Brewer
Assistant Editor: J. Ben Wiles
Chief Copy Editor, Layout, and Design: Lenae Simmons

PREFACE

How to Start a Living What We Believe Group

The following steps are important in the process of starting a group in your local church:

1. Pray and seek the leadership of the Holy Spirit to make sure He is calling you to lead a Living What We Believe group.

2. Secure permission from the pastor of your local church to lead the group.

3. Find an appropriate location that is conducive to the group encounters—either in the church facility or in a host home. Public areas such as coffee shops are not appropriate, as they would potentially hinder the group's ability to fully engage the leading of the Spirit during times of prayer.

4. Set a time and place for the first meeting.

5. Develop the group through invitation. Your goal is clear: to lead every member of the group to grow in Jesus Christ, and to discover and fulfill God's personal call on his or her life in the power

of the Holy Spirit. This is a transformation group where every member will grow and be fully involved in the discipleship process personally and by leading others in the discipleship process. Select four or, at most, five people to be in your group. Include at least one mature believer and at least one new believer. (Note: a group with four to five people is best for a study such as this one. However, if you need to have a larger group, you should not have more than 10 to 12 people).

6. Decide how you are going to handle childcare.

7. Determine the cost for the group. Group members should purchase their own copy of the student guides for each unit, unless the church has opted to make other arrangements.

8. Order materials in plenty of time to have them for the first group encounter.

9. Read through the leader's guide and acclimate yourself to the Living What We Believe discipleship process.

Keys to Successfully Leading a Small Group

1. Get to know the group members.

2. Encourage participation by everyone. Remember that discipleship and lecturing are not the same thing. You are a facilitator, and your job is to facilitate participation that leads to transformation for everyone!

   - Communicate your expectation that everyone participates.

   - Ask questions.

   - Make it fulfilling so they want to return.

   - Reduce and eliminate embarrassing and threatening situations.

   - Protect and honor confidentiality within the group.

3. Affirming vs. Endorsing

   - It is important that, as the leader, you affirm all the responses. You say, "Thank you, Ben," or "That's very interesting, Elizabeth." No matter what the participants say, don't criticize their remarks. What they just said may be antagonistic to you or it may simply sound ridiculous, but don't directly criticize it. Instead, say something like, "Well, that's interesting. What do the rest of you think?" Once you, as the leader, directly disapprove of someone's comments, then some people will never speak up again. They're going to fear disapproval; once exploration stops for them, the journey does too. On the other side of the coin, while it's important to affirm all responses, avoid the temptation to endorse them. Don't say things like, "Now that's a great comment," or "I couldn't agree with you more." Such endorsements tip your hand and leave others feeling like their comments are not acceptable. Also, resist the urge to be too instructional, trying to answer everyone's questions and solve everyone's problems. Once a know-it-all person speaks up, conversation tends to shut down. You can give your own opinion, but do it in a personal and humble way. Maybe you could say, "My experience has been . . ." or "This is how I see it . . ."

4. Remember the four C's of the facilitator's role:

- **Content**—Keep the group grounded in Scripture.

- **Care**—Be sensitive to the feelings, needs, and life situations of the group members.

- **Commitment**—Demonstrate your commitment to completing the Living What We Believe process completely and thoroughly. Model your commitment by your careful preparation as the facilitator for each of the group encounters.

- **Consistency**—Follow up consistently with established schedules and routines for the group. Your consistent approach to the process will inspire the same in the participants. Also, a consistently positive attitude will go a long way to establishing a healthy environment for the group to flourish.

5. Manage difficult and challenging personalities in your group so they don't hijack the encounters.

   - The Talking Hijacker answers every question before anyone else can respond. In her book, *Help! My Small Group Has Been Hijacked!, Four Common Hijackers and ways to Respond*, Margaret Feinberg discusses helpful responses to potential small group "Hijackings."

     o Your first course of action is to pull them aside in a one-on-one meeting. Thank them for their participation, but be honest with them about the need for others to participate. Consider some practical ways you could offer to help them do that (respond only to every second or third question, keep responses short, and so forth).

o Your second course of action (if the first course of action doesn't work) is to change the discussion time to a more structured format. For example, you call on people for answers.

- The Emotional Hijacker shows up every week with an emotional crisis.

o The first course of action is to spend some one-on-one time with this person and allow him or her to emotionally unpack with you. If necessary, recommend a good counselor or a conversation with the pastor. This may alleviate the problem in the group encounter.

o If the first course of action doesn't resolve the issue, you may need to remind the group of the task at hand, which is to work through the material, and that extra questions can be raised at the end of the session.

- ○ **Note**: there may be a person in your group who is just going through a difficult time and is not truly an emotional hijacker. Be open to the leading of the Holy Spirit to allow a short time of personal ministry to this person if you feel it is appropriate; then return to the material at hand for that group encounter.

6. The Leader Hijacker is a backseat driver who is constantly making suggestions about how you should lead the group.

- • The first course of action is to have a one-on-one conversation with the individual. Sift through his or her comments to see if you can glean anything helpful. Sometimes, there will be good suggestions that can benefit the group. If so, mention these helpful suggestions in your conversation, which will keep the atmosphere positive. Politely ask the leader hijacker to stop doing so at the group encounters by pointing out that he/she can lead to disunity in the group.

- • If the hijacker does it in another meeting, simply say, "We can talk about suggestions outside of the group encounter," then continue with the material at hand.

7. The Late Hijacker constantly walks into the group encounter late, disrupting the group and causing a loss of momentum and focus.

- Discuss the situation directly with the individual and encourage him or her to make every effort to arrive on time. If that is not possible, encourage him or her to arrive quietly and discreetly so as to not disturb the group. They should also consider waiting outside if it seems to be a particularly sensitive moment.

- If the individual continues to disrupt the group, consider privately encouraging them to find another group to join that would work better with his or her schedule.

8. Remember, you are accountable for your stewardship of the group!

- Care for them enough that you refuse to accept poor decisions or justification for inconsistent participation.

- Don't be judgmental. Address behaviors only—don't try to guess the motivation behind them.

- Pray regularly over the group.

- See yourself as a mentor/role model.

- Encourage authentic relationships and conversations in the group by modeling them. Be yourself and be real, but also be holy and be humble!

- Trust God. Whatever is accomplished is by Him and through Him and for His glory. It is His will for you and your group to succeed and He is ready to give you the grace to do so!

Group Covenant

Instead, speaking the truth in love, we will grow to become in every respect the mature body of him who is the head, that is, Christ. From him the whole body, joined and held together by every supporting ligament, grows and builds itself up in love, as each part does its work (Ephesians 4:15-16 NIV).

It is hoped that each individual undertaking the Living What We Believe process will experience transformation and growth in Christlikeness over the course of the experience. But individual growth alone is not enough. It must take place in the context of relationship with others of the same faith, each one building the others up so that all become mature followers of Jesus Christ and, as a result, fully functioning participants in God's plan to save creation. With that in mind, before continuing with the study, each member of the group should agree to the following covenant with one another. Please read and reflect upon the following statements and indicate your commitment to the group by signing your name at the bottom. Then each member of the Living What We Believe group should sign one another's group covenant so that everyone's copy has every signature of the group. Keep this group covenant in your book for future reference as needed.

GROUP COVENANT

PRIORITY: The group meeting will be a priority in my schedule. If I am running late or unable to attend, I will contact my group leader.

PREPAREDNESS: I realize that what I put into the lesson is what I will get out of it. Therefore, I will prepare for the lesson each week and come prepared to share.

RESPECT: Everyone has a right to his or her opinion and all questions are encouraged and respected. I will listen attentively to others without interrupting them.

CONFIDENTIALITY: Anything of a personal nature that is said in the meeting should not be repeated outside the meeting. This group is intended to be a safe place for open discussion and sharing.

HONESTY: I will strive to be real, honest, and transparent with the other group members.

SUPPORT: The mission and values of the group have my support, and I will refrain from gossip or criticism.

SIGNATURES   DATE

A SPIRIT-BAPTIZED PEOPLE

Introduction

The focus of this series of studies about the *Declaration of Faith* is how we can come to *know, be,* and *do* the truth of the gospel, that is, how we can live fully in the good news of God's love. We live in love in all areas of life through the grace of Jesus Christ and the call, counsel, and empowerment of the Holy Spirit. As we walk in God's ways, we grow in faith by continually allowing His Spirit to renew our passion. To experience this renewal, it is important for us to study God's Word regularly and to invite the revitalizing presence of the Holy Spirit into our lives and churches.

Our focus for this study. In this study, we will focus our attention on the particular experience and work of the Holy Spirit that is often referred to by various names: *baptism (in, with,* or *of) the Holy Spirit (or the Holy Ghost), Spirit baptism, infilling of the Holy Spirit,* or *being filled with the Holy Spirit.* In modern times, this move of the Spirit has also been referred to as the *Pentecostal experience*, since Jesus' disciples experienced this move of the Holy Spirit on the Day of Pentecost, and it is an experience common within the Pentecostal Movement.

The Holy Spirit. One question that we might hear today within the Pentecostal Movement and churches is: "*Do we see and experience the Holy Spirit moving in our churches and lives today?*" As we consider this question, it is important to begin with a basic understanding about who the Holy Spirit is.

The Holy Spirit is the third person of the Trinity and is equal to the Father and Son. The Spirit is God, and like the Father and the Son, knows all things, is all-powerful, and is everywhere. The Holy Spirit dwells in every Christian from the moment of conversion.

The Holy Spirit, sent by the Father in Jesus' name (as Jesus' representative), continually refreshes and revives the church today. Through this spiritual renewal, the Spirit helps the church live out its call of love—that is, to express the love of Jesus through words and actions in both the church and the world.

Throughout this study, to help us understand and experience the Holy Spirit more fully, we will explore: what we can learn from the Spirit-filled church in the Book of Acts about the move and empowerment of the

Holy Spirit, and how we can become open to the move of the Spirit in our lives and in the life of the church.

The Pentecostal Movement's experience and teachings about baptism in the Holy Spirit. The modern *Pentecostal Movement* had its beginning at the turn of twentieth century. The biblical roots of this movement are the Book of Acts and particularly chapter 2, which records that the disciples of Jesus received the baptism in (infilling with) the Spirit. *Baptism in the Spirit* may be defined as an experience that is received after salvation in which the Holy Spirit, the third person of the Godhead, comes upon believers and empowers them for special service for living the Christian life. Accompanying this experience is *speaking in tongues* (technically known as *glossolalia*, consisting of two Greek words: *glossa*—tongues and *lalia*—speaking). Pentecostal churches teach that speaking in tongues is the initial evidence of the baptism in the Spirit. At times, this manifestation is referred to as *the initial physical evidence, the initial sign,* or *the first oral evidence.*

Baptism in the Spirit is a total submersion of one's own spirit in the Holy Spirit. Those who receive this experience find themselves surrounded, covered, and filled with the presence of God. Similar to a garment that has been dipped in water, they are saturated with the Spirit of God. To be *baptized in the Spirit* is to have an overwhelming and intense experience in the Holy Spirit.

The Bible. The baptism in the Spirit first occurred on the Day of Pentecost after Jesus ascended into heaven. On that occasion, the disciples were baptized in/filled with the Holy Spirit. Their baptism was accompanied by visible and audible manifestations, such as a sound from heaven, tongues like fire, and speaking in tongues (Acts 2:1-4). Likewise, Luke relates that when Jesus was baptized by John in the Jordan River, His experience was both visible and audible. As Jesus was being baptized in water, "the Holy Spirit descended in bodily form like a dove upon Him, and a voice came from heaven which said, 'You are My beloved Son; in You I am well pleased'" (Luke 3:22). Just as audible and visible signs were evidence of Jesus' anointing by the Spirit, audible and visible signs on the Day of Pentecost confirmed the disciples' baptism in the Spirit. Peter spoke of the experience as being an experience in which the crowd could both "see and hear" (Acts 2:33).

Scripture teaches:

1. When a person makes a decision to follow Jesus Christ, experiencing *salvation*, the Holy Spirit comes to dwell in that individual (*indwelling*). That person receives the *fruit of the Spirit*, and the Spirit's comfort and guidance for living (Romans 8:9; Galatians 5:22-23; Ephesians 1:13).

2. Later, when a person experiences *baptism in the Holy Spirit*, that person is *immersed* in and experiences a full, overflowing blessing of the Spirit. This experience is a special anointing, a filling up (*infilling*) with spiritual empowerment for service and life. Speaking in tongues is an important part of this experience of being baptized in the Holy Spirit.

Evidence of baptism of the Spirit. The idea of tongues as being the *initial evidence* of the fullness of the Spirit emphasizes that the infilling of the Spirit has been experienced. Therefore, the term *initial* refers to the immediate, physical outward expression of the person being baptized in the Spirit, The word *evidence* points to tongues as being the sign of confirmation of spiritual empowerment subsequent to receiving salvation. In other words, speaking in tongues is the immediate, visible, and audible sign that the baptism in the Spirit has been received.

Even though the initial evidence and speaking in other tongues have been major aspects of Pentecostal belief, we know from the Bible that speaking in tongues is not the whole story. In addition to this particular manifestation of the Holy Spirit, the Scriptures also speak about continuing and ongoing evidence of the Spirit in a person's life. This evidence includes life choices such as: commitment to witnessing for Jesus Christ, commitment to the whole truth of the Bible, commitment to Christian fellowship and worship, and commitment to bearing the fruit of the Spirit in all of life. Therefore, we should value all the evidences of the Holy Spirit and not minimize any of them. The audible manifestations of the Spirit at the time of our baptism in the Spirit are very important.

In light of the bewildered response on the Day of Pentecost, we know that this oral manifestation is deeply mysterious and can be controversial. On the Day of Pentecost, people wanted to know how it was that they could hear Galileans speaking their own language, the language into which they were born (Acts 2:7-8). Others mocked and said, "'They are full of new wine'" (v. 13). God's ways are sometimes very mysterious. It is important for us to trust God and His ways and timing, and to support and encourage each other through our questions and efforts to understand Him and the work of His Spirit.

Baptism in the Spirit—a personal experience. This brief introduction indicates that the baptism in the Spirit is a highly personal experience. As already stated, the Scriptures give us direction for understanding and receiving this Pentecostal blessing. The spiritual experience and teachings of the early Christians provide the present-day Church with models for receiving all that God has for us and for living a life pleasing to God.

Those who read and study this book may have different backgrounds and views of the baptism in the Spirit. As a student of God's Word, you may be a new Christian or new to the Pentecostal church. Maybe you are unfamiliar with some of the teachings of the Bible, or possibly even are bewildered or confused by particular Pentecostal teachings about baptism in the Spirit and speaking in tongues. On the other hand, you may feel like you understand this material and have experienced the fullness of the Spirit. It is hoped that those who have questions will feel free to ask them, and that those who have experienced baptism in the Holy Spirit will through their personal testimony, fellowship, and prayer help their friends to also understand and experience the fullness of the Spirit. It is my prayer that as you begin this study, you will grow in understanding and in your daily walk with the Holy Spirit.

My Testimony. I can tell you that I was among those who had virtually no understanding of Spirit baptism when I received the experience. I served in the Army during the Korean War. After two years in Okinawa, I came home. At that time, my mother was attending a small Pentecostal church, and I was unsaved. The church had begun a revival, and the first night I went to the revival, God touched my heart and graciously forgave my sins. The people who had prayed with me around the altar told me that God wanted to do more in my life.

7

They talked about being filled with Spirit, but I had no idea what they meant. I had no real understanding about the Spirit, but the next night when the evangelist invited the congregation to come and pray, I knelt at the altar not knowing what to expect.

Suddenly, the Holy Spirit came upon me, and I felt surrounded by the presence of the Lord. I was overwhelmed with an intense feeling of joy, and I was praising the Lord in a language that I did not know. I had no understanding of what had happened until the evangelist explained that I had been filled with the Spirit and that the tongues were the sign of that experience. I will never doubt the reality of that experience.

DECLARATION OF FAITH

◆◆◆◆◆◆◆

"*We Believe . . .*

In the baptism with the Holy Ghost subsequent to a clean heart."

"*We Believe . . .*

In speaking with other tongues as the Spirit gives utterance and that it is the initial evidence of the baptism of the Holy Ghost."

OUTPOURING

OF THE

HOLY SPIRIT

Week 1

Day 1

Jerusalem on the Day of Pentecost

DECLARATION OF FAITH

"We Believe . . .

In the baptism with the Holy Ghost subsequent to a clean heart."

"We Believe . . .

In speaking with other tongues as the Spirit gives utterance and that it is the initial evidence of the baptism of the Holy Ghost."

Words to Hide in Your Heart

But you shall receive power when the Holy Spirit has come upon you; and you shall be witnesses to Me in Jerusalem, and in all Judea and Samaria, and to the end of the earth (Acts 1:8).

And they were all filled with the Holy Spirit and began to speak with other tongues, as the Spirit gave them the utterance (2:4).

Touching Base

Our focus this week as we begin this study is on the first outpouring of the Spirit on the Christian church. This outpouring provided the basis for the church to preach the gospel (the good news about Jesus) to the world. On this occasion, the disciples received the same power for preaching the gospel and performing miracles as Jesus did at the Jordan River.

Searching the Scripture

Read Acts 2:1-4:

When the Day of Pentecost had fully come, they were all with one accord in one place. And suddenly there came a sound from heaven, as of a rushing mighty wind, and it filled the whole house where they were sitting. Then there appeared to them divided tongues, as of fire, and one sat upon each of them. And they were all filled with the Holy

Spirit and began to speak with other tongues, as the Spirit gave them utterance.

Answer the Following Questions:

1. What was the "Day of Pentecost"? (See "*Know*" section below.)

2. Who were present when the Holy Spirit arrived? Where were they? Why were they there? What were they doing? What happened?

3. What do you think it means to be "*with one accord*"? (See Acts 2:1.)

4. On the Day of Pentecost, what were the audible and visible signs that the Holy Spirit was present, and that the followers of Christ had been filled with the Spirit?

5. What did other people who observed the happenings that day experience? (See 2:5-21.)

6. What are some similarities between Jesus' experience at the Jordan River (Luke 3:21-22) and the experience of the 120 believers on the Day of Pentecost? (See Acts 2:1-4.) How do we know from these accounts that Jesus was a man of the Spirit and the 120 were people of the Spirit?

7. Have you experienced the power of the Holy Spirit in your life? In the life of the church?

Yielding to the Spirit

—*Know*—

The Feast of Pentecost. The first outpouring of the Holy Spirit on the Christian church occurred in Jerusalem on the *Day of Pentecost* (Acts 2:1-4). In biblical times, *Pentecost* was a harvest (firstfruits) festival in which Jews traveled to Jerusalem to give thanks and to present offerings of new grain at the Temple (Exodus 23:14-16; 34:22; Leviticus 23:16-17).

The Hebrew name for this festival was *Feast of Weeks* (*Shavuot*–meaning *weeks* or *sevens*); the Greeks referred to it as *Pentecost* (*Pentekoste*–meaning *fifty*). Both these names came from the fact that it was observed on the fiftieth day at the end of a seven-week counting period. This counting period followed another "*wave offering*," which was observed in connection with *Passover* and the *Feast of Unleavened Bread* (Leviticus 23:4-22; Deuteronomy 16:1-12, 16).

Later the Feast of Weeks/Pentecost came to be a time in which Jewish people also commemorated the giving of *the Law* (*the Torah*) to Moses at Mt. Sinai (Exodus 24:12). Today both Jews and Christians continue to observe *Shavuot* and *Pentecost.* On Shavuot, Jews give thanks to God for His provision, and renew their acceptance of His gift of the Torah. On Pentecost, Christians give thanks to God for the gift of the Holy Spirit. Christians celebrate Pentecost seven weeks after Easter Sunday, on the fiftieth day, at the conclusion of the Easter Season.

Need for empowerment from the Holy Spirit. As instructed by Jesus, during the time of the Pentecost festival, His disciples had come to Jerusalem to wait for the promised Holy Spirit. These followers of Jesus who came to Jerusalem were already Christians. They had been saved through the grace of Jesus Christ, and the Holy Spirit had come to dwell in them at the time that they had put their faith in Jesus as their Savior. *Please note:* It is evident from Paul's words in Romans that the Holy Spirit dwells in all Christians from the beginning of their walk with Christ: "Now if anyone does not have the Spirit of Christ, he is not His" (Romans 8:9).

Even though the disciples were saved (rescued from sin and its darkness, and given new life) and were indwelt by the Holy Spirit, they had not yet received the deeper experience in the Spirit. Jesus told them to stay in Jerusalem until they received the promise of the Holy Spirit, who would enable them to become bold witnesses "to the end of the earth" (Acts 1:4-5, 8). While "to the end of the earth" may have meant for Jesus' disciples the city of Rome, this commission embraced the whole of humankind and the focus of this promise and call is on the worldwide mission of the church to spread the gospel, that is to share the good news about the love of Jesus Christ and God's forgiveness and saving grace.

In order to be "witnesses" about Jesus, the disciples needed to be equipped to speak confidently and effectively about Jesus' death and resurrection, even in the face of danger. So, Jesus promised to give them supernatural power to carry the message of the gospel and to serve. This power that Jesus promised was not political power or power to rule, but power to serve and share His good news with others. This kind of power was received by the early believers through the baptism of the Spirit on the Day of Pentecost. Jesus' disciples are wonderful models for believers today. All believers need the power that the disciples received on the Day of Pentecost.

The disciples' experience during Pentecost. As the disciples were waiting and praying in Jerusalem, they were filled with the Spirit. A multitude of devout Jews were there from various countries celebrating the feast of Pentecost. Two signs—a mighty sound like wind from heaven and the dividing of tongues similar to fire— occurred. These signs marked the greatness of this occasion in which God was doing something new. The two signs were not part of later outpourings of the Spirit recorded in the Book of Acts (8:14-19; 9:15-19; 10:44-46; 19:1-7). But speaking in tongues, a visible, audible sign that occurred on that day indicated the disciples had been filled with Spirit. The occurrence of tongues was a reoccurring experience in later outpourings of the Spirit (Acts 10:44-46; 19:1-7). On the occasion of Acts 2:5-6, the Galilean disciples spoke in the native languages of the onlookers (a Holy Spirit-inspired special form of speaking in languages not known by the speakers, but known by the multitude present—*zenolalia*— foreign languages).

The Last Days. Having been filled with the Spirit, Peter preached his great Pentecostal sermon (Acts 2:14-41). In it, he links the miraculous events of Pentecost to Joel 2:28-32. In the beginning of his Spirit-inspired sermon, Peter tells the people that the disciples are not drunk as supposed, that they had been filled with Spirit, which was to be poured out on "all flesh" as Joel had predicted. The "*last days*" mentioned in Joel's prophecy had been initiated by the first coming of Christ into the world and the outpouring of the Spirit at Pentecost. Since that time, the church has lived in the last days.

There will come the last of the last days; then there will come the Day of the Lord, which will be preceded by signs such as wars, fire, hail, and the coloring of the moon.

Many of these signs will be indications of the terrible things that will occur in the earth and heaven before Christ comes again. Before Christ returns is the time to carry the gospel "to the end of the earth" (Acts 1:8). Through the baptism in the Holy Spirit, God provides His people with the mighty power of the Spirit to bear witness to the gospel until the second coming of Christ.

The Holy Spirit in the Church Today:

- *The Holy Spirit has always respected the freedom of believers and has sought their cooperation.* When the 120 believers were baptized (immersed) in the Holy Spirit, their speech was inspired, not forced on them by the Spirit. The disciples and other believers willingly spoke, as they allowed the Holy Spirit to inspire them. Through the Spirit's empowerment, their words were mighty and authoritative and served as the outward sign that they had received the fullness of the Spirit.

- *The coming of the Holy Spirit provided power to the early church, and also provides power to us to take the gospel (God's good news) into the world.* As we see in the Book of Acts, this outpouring of the Spirit was the first of a series of advances for the church. God still empowers His people to spread the gospel in ever widening circles.

- *Language inspired by the Holy Spirit can serve as both a sign of an individual's experience in the baptism in the Holy Spirit, as well as for the spiritual benefit of others.* The disciples' speaking in other languages was a sign to them of the power of the Holy Spirit in their own lives, and was also a confirmation to others about the power of the One the disciples served, Jesus Christ. Still today, this spiritual sign shows the reality and power of God to those who may not believe, or may have doubts, that God is truly present and active in the world (1 Corinthians 14:22).

- *The Holy Spirit's invitation to Jesus Christ.* The Holy Spirit's presence, which is proclaimed through this sign, may also serve as a convicting call to those who already consider themselves godly, believing people. On the Day of Pentecost, inspired by this spiritual sign, Peter declared a message about the identity of Jesus for the benefit of the religious leaders in the crowd and their followers. Peter said: "let all the house of Israel know assuredly that God has made this Jesus, whom you crucified, both Lord and Christ" (Acts 2:36). Peter's Spirit-inspired words served as an invitation to those present, and they "were cut to the heart, and said to Peter and the rest of the apostles, 'Men and brethren, what shall we do?'" (v. 37).

The experiences and words shared on the Day of Pentecost are also signs and invitations to us today—to come to Jesus Christ, and open ourselves to the blessings of the Holy Spirit.

—Be—

Unity among the followers of Jesus. The followers of the risen Jesus Christ were united in their obedience to His instructions, which were to remain in Jerusalem and to pray and wait for the promised Holy Spirit. After praying ten days, they were filled with the joy and vigor of the Holy Spirit, speaking in inspired words, and becoming inspired prophets with the ability and strength to share the good news of Jesus Christ with the world (Joel 2:28-32; Acts 1:4-14; 2:1-4).

Consider:

- What might it mean for you and your church fellowship, to wait on God and His Holy Spirit?

- How might you wait on the Lord and the Holy Spirit in your own personal devotion time?

- As the Holy Spirit blesses you, what might you expect to happen in your heart and life?

- How do you feel about the fact that the Holy Spirit moves according to God's will and timing, and no one can know how the Spirit might move? Is this a risk worth taking? If so, why?

—*Do*—

The anointing of the Holy Spirit. As we have seen in the Book of Acts, God wants to empower His people to carry into the world the good news about Jesus Christ and God's love and grace, which He expresses through His Son Jesus. Just as Jesus was obedient to God's will in His baptism, and the disciples were obedient to Jesus when they stayed in Jerusalem to wait on the Holy Spirit, so we are to be obedient.

The actions of the followers of Jesus, as recorded in Acts 2, are good examples for us. Like the disciples, as we pray and trust in God, we can experience the Holy Spirit's anointing, too. Through this anointing, we can receive strength, courage, and guidance.

The Great Commission. When the Holy Spirit fills us to overflowing, we will experience inward and outward miracles as God wills, such as audible and visual signs and wonders, clarity of calling, and a level of love, joy, and peace that can only come from God. May the church continually be open to God's miracles manifested through the Holy Spirit as we endeavor to carry out His *Great Commission* (that is, His call to us to be representatives of Jesus, taking His love to the world).

Offer a Prayer

Heavenly Father, You fill us with good things. I ask now for You to fill me with Your Holy Spirit. I want to be totally immersed, baptized in the presence of God. I want to overflow with the Spirit's love, wisdom, and strength so that I may share Your love with others. Amen.

Day 2

Samaria

Searching the Scripture

Read Acts 8:14-17:

> Now when the apostles who were at Jerusalem heard that Samaria had received the word of God, they sent Peter and John to them, who, when they had come down, prayed for them that they might receive the Holy Spirit. For as yet He had fallen upon none of them. They had only been baptized in the name of the Lord Jesus. Then they laid hands on them, and they received the Holy Spirit.

Answer the Following Questions:

1. Read Acts 8:1-25.

2. Why do you think Luke in his narrative in the Book of Acts focuses on an experience in which believers are empowered for service—an experience that occurs after the point in which believers invite Jesus and His love into their hearts and lives?

3. What do you think that Simon, the magician, saw that made him want the ability to give to others the power of the Spirit? (See Acts 8:18-24).

4. What is the difference between understanding *speaking in tongues* as an end in themselves and understanding them as initial evidence of being filled with the Spirit's power for serving God?

Yielding to the Spirit

—Know—

Samaritans dedicate their lives to Jesus. The encounter of the Samaritans with the Holy Spirit is a striking story. On one occasion, Philip, one of the Spirit-filled deacons (Acts 6:5) and a gifted evangelist (21:8), had travelled to Samaria. While there, the genuineness of his ministry was confirmed by great miracles, the Samaritans believed his preaching, and were baptized in water by him as a sign that their sins had been forgiven. These Samaritans, while they had received the indwelling presence of the Holy Spirit when they decided to accept the love of Jesus and follow Him, did not receive the fullness of the Spirit until sometime later. In fact, the Spirit did not fall on them until after Peter and John arrived from Jerusalem.

Samaritans receive the Holy Spirit. Peter and John, when they heard that "Samaria had received the word of God," travelled to Samaria. Upon arriving there, they learned that none of the Samaritan Christians had received the baptism in the Spirit. So Peter and John prayed and laid hands on them, and the Samaritans received the powerful anointing of the Spirit (8:14-17). Their experience of the Holy Spirit occurred after they had accepted the good news about Jesus and had been baptized in water. This is a striking example of *the doctrine of subsequence*, an intense empowering encounter with the Holy Spirit that is distinct and separate from one's saving encounter with Jesus.

Supernatural signs and miracles. Luke does not give all the details, in fact, he makes no direct mention of the Samaritans' speaking in tongues, but the manifestation that occurred when Peter and John prayed for the Samaritans convinced Simon, a magician who was present, that these believers had received the power of the Spirit. Simon had already seen miracles that had accompanied the ministry of Philip (8:5-8, 13). However, this time what most likely convinced him that there was a special power from which he could benefit was that when Peter and John laid hands on people, they had a supernatural experience. Simon would have witnessed some visible, audible sign, which would have been *speaking in tongues* (vv. 17-19). This audible, visible sign fit the occasion. It demonstrated the supernatural presence and empowerment of the Holy Spirit.

—Be—

The people of Samaria were open to the love of Jesus, miracles, and blessings from the Holy Spirit.

a) The Samaritans believed Philip when he preached about the kingdom of God and who Jesus Christ was (8:12, 14).

b) The Samaritans, both men and women, were baptized in water in the name of the Lord Jesus (vv. 12, 16).

c) The apostles prayed for the Samaritans, then "they received the Holy Spirit" (vv. 14-17).

d) The Ethiopian received the joy of salvation when he: listened to Philip's teaching and preaching about Jesus, believed with all his heart, was baptized in water, then witnessed the Spirit of the Lord taking Philip away (vv. 26-40).

Consider:

- How might the people discussed in the passages above be marvelous examples for us?

- As you think about these passages, consider if you also welcome the unconditional love, acceptance, and forgiveness that Jesus is offering you today?

- You may want to ask God to help you receive the love of Jesus—and the Holy Spirit's blessings, guidance, and strength.

—Do—

The good news for all the world. Having been filled with the Spirit, Philip went about sharing the good news with others. He brought great joy to the Samaritan believers. A crucial significance of his preaching the gospel in Samaria was not the number people who came to the Lord, but that it was the first step of the church in taking the good news to the world.

The gospel—the good news—that you share with others, as Philip did, will bring to their hearts a joy they have never known.

Consider:

- Explore ideas for how you might communicate through both actions and words the truths of God's love that can be experienced through Jesus Christ and the presence of the Holy Spirit.

- What is a first step you can take to share this Good news with someone in your life?

- Are there any people you know who might like for you to tell them about your experiences with Jesus and the Holy Spirit, and to pray for them?

Offer a Prayer

Father, through Your Holy Spirit, show me how I might share Your good news about the love of Jesus with those You send my way. As I care and pray for others, help me to be humble and to focus on You rather than giving glory to myself. In the name of Jesus, My Lord, I pray. Amen.

Day 3

Caesarea

Searching the Scripture

Read Acts 10:44-46:

> While Peter was still speaking these words, the Holy Spirit fell upon all those who heard the word. And those of the circumcision who believed were astonished, as many as came with Peter, because the gift of the Holy Spirit had been poured out on the Gentiles also. For they heard them speak with tongues and magnify God.

Answer the Following Questions:

1. Read Acts 10:1-48 and 11:1-18.

2. Why did Cornelius, who was a Gentile and officer of the Italian Regiment of the Roman army, send a delegation of men to Simon Peter, a Jewish follower of Jesus? (See Acts 10:1-8, 30-33.)

3. When the men sent by Cornelius arrived in Joppa, why did Peter extend hospitality to them, then the next day travel with them and some of his own friends to Caesarea (Acts 10:9-23)? What word from God did Peter receive through the Spirit (v. 19)? Note: At that time, a devout Jew would not normally visit in the home of a non-Jew because he would become ritually "unclean," disqualifying him for worship in the Temple.

4. When Peter arrived in Caesarea, to whom did he speak? What did Peter talk about (what words from God did he give them)? What happened while Peter was speaking? (See Acts 10:24-29, 34-48.)

5. When the Gentiles in Caesarea spoke in tongues, the tongues showed they had been immersed in the fullness of the Holy Spirit, and that they had also been accepted into the family of God (Acts 10:44-48). Later when Peter went to Jerusalem, he was questioned about the inclusion of Gentiles (non-Jews) in the church. How did Peter defend his decision to share "the word of God" (the gospel) with non-Jews? What manifestations from God did he mention in his explanation?

6. "The Holy Spirit"/"the Spirit" is mentioned several times in the story about Peter and Cornelius. What are those occurrences?

7. What are some similarities and differences between the outpouring of the Holy Spirit in Jerusalem on the Day of Pentecost (Acts chapter 2) and the Spirit's appearance in Caesarea at the home of Cornelius? (See chapter 10.)

8. How does this story about Peter and Cornelius demonstrate: that no race is better than any other, and that God loves *all* people from *all* nations and religious backgrounds—that God loves everyone equally?

Yielding to the Spirit

—Know—

The Holy Spirit and Cornelius, and Peter. Cornelius was a Gentile and a rough Roman soldier. However, he was a man of prayer and known for his generosity. At this time among Jewish followers of Jesus, there was still the issue of accepting Gentiles into the church. God prepared Peter (Simon Peter) to go to Caesarea and to welcome the Gentile Cornelius and his family and friends—into the body of Christ. While Peter was staying at the home of Simon, the tanner, in Joppa, he had a vision. As he was pondering what the vision meant, messengers arrived from Cornelius. The Spirit told Peter to go with them to Caesarea (Acts 10:19).

There is some discussion about whether Cornelius had become a Christian before Peter's arrival or as Peter preached to Cornelius and his friends, they became Christians and soon afterwards were filled with the Spirit.
Either way, Cornelius and others were filled with the Holy Spirit, which was evident because they spoke in tongues.

The outpouring of the Spirit in Caesarea compared to the outpouring in Jerusalem. The similarities between the outpouring of the Spirit in Jerusalem and Caesarea are striking. Both the Jewish believers in Jerusalem and the Gentile believers in Caesarea were filled with the Spirit, and they spoke in tongues (2:4; 10:44-46) and praised and honored God (2:11; 10:46). As these passages indicate, through the inspiration of the Spirit, tongues can include praise and give thanksgiving to God for His mighty acts that are recorded in the Old Testament and His blessings that He gives through Jesus Christ (1 Corinthians 14:2, 14-15). No doubt, the magnifying and praising of God are closely related to the observable, audible manifestation of the Holy Spirit.

In Caesarea, this outward, audible sign of speaking in tongues convinced Peter and the six Jewish Christians ("*brethren*") with him that the Gentiles had been received into the family of God. Later, Peter testified in Jerusalem to Jewish followers of Christ, that God had given the Holy Spirit to Cornelius (a Gentile), "just as He did to us" (Acts 15:8).

God's love for all people. At the beginning of his sermon in Caesarea, Peter had spoken about how God had changed his attitude toward the Gentiles: "In truth I perceive that God shows no partiality. But in every nation, whoever fears Him and works righteousness is accepted by Him" [that is, in every nation, whoever honors God and is willing to do what is right (willing to live in agreement with God's love), is accepted and welcomed by Him] (10:34-35). Peter's vision in Joppa had convinced Him that God has no favorites. Also, the spiritual manifestation that occurred as Peter preached clearly indicated that the overwhelming presence and power of the Holy Spirit were at work in the lives of the Gentile believers.

—*Be*—

Answering God's call. This story about Peter and Cornelius shows how our obedience to the Word of God and His love can break down walls of religious and racial prejudice and bring about new life and new relationships. Since a large amount of space in the Book of Acts is devoted to this story, we can conclude that it must be very important.

In this account, God spoke to both a Jewish man and a Gentile. God's words were delivered through: visions, words from the Holy Spirit, and Peter's Spirit-inspired actions and speech. Peter's and Cornelius' obedience to God's instructions resulted in Cornelius' family and friends experiencing the love of Jesus Christ and the outpouring of the Holy Spirit.

Consider:

- During a time of reflection and prayer, ask the Holy Spirit to show you what lessons you can learn from the account of Peter and Cornelius.

- What do you think of the statement: *We are not haters of people unlike us, but we are healers of the racial-divide?*

- What could being a healer of the racial-divide mean for your life? For the life of the church?

—*Do*—

Loving our neighbors across the culture's barriers. Peter knew the love of Christ and had been filled with the Spirit at Pentecost, but he needed more spiritual insight and awakening to deal with his religious and racial prejudices. In this story, both Peter and Cornelius were open to listening to God's instructions and teaching, even though these instructions were outside the cultural norms. The results were that they gained new, healing perspectives, grew spiritually, developed new relationships, and their lives and the life of the church were changed for the better.

Daily wisdom and empowerment through the Holy Spirit. It is important that no matter how long we have been Christians or how powerful our experiences with the Holy Spirit have been, that we remain open to the voice of God (God's word) through the Scriptures and the move of the Spirit. As we are attentive to and act on God's Word, we will be able to experience more fully the blessings of the Holy Spirit and will be more able to communicate the love of Jesus with others. Our "Pentecost" experience should become a dynamic, ever-present reality in which we are aware daily of the presence, guidance, and empowerment of the Spirit.

Expressing God's love to others. It is clear from today's reading that the Holy Spirit calls believers to leave the comforts of the familiar to show hospitality and share God's good news with others. We can see from God's Word and encounters with the Holy Spirit on the Day of Pentecost and at the home of Cornelius, that we are to love all people. We are not only to love all our neighbors as ourselves, but also we are to go a step further and love them as Jesus has loved us (Leviticus 19:18; Matthew 22:39; Luke 10:25-37; John 13:34).

Consider:

- How might you respectfully show love and hospitality to one person or family—maybe someone of a different nationality, culture, race, religion, lifestyle, or life circumstance?

- How might the church do this?

- What do you think the church can do to address prejudices that occur within the church and the community?

Offer a Prayer

Heavenly Father, You love all people. Through the wisdom and power of the Holy Spirit, show me how to love as my Lord Jesus loves, to release any prejudices I may have, and to be an instrument of Your healing and reconciliation in the church and world. Amen.

Day 4

Ephesus

Searching the Scripture

Read Acts 19:1-7:

> And it happened, while Apollos was at Corinth, that Paul, having passed through the upper regions, came to Ephesus. And finding some disciples he said to them, "Did you receive the Holy Spirit when you believed?" So they said to him, "We have not so much as heard whether there is a Holy Spirit." And he said to them, "Into what then were you baptized?" So they said, "Into John's baptism." Then Paul said, "John indeed baptized with a baptism of repentance, saying to the people that they should believe on Him who would come after him, that is, on Christ Jesus." When they heard this, they were baptized in the name of the Lord Jesus. And when Paul had laid hands on them, the Holy Spirit came upon them, and they spoke with tongues and prophesied. Now the men were about twelve in all.

Answer the Following Questions:

1. From the account recorded in Acts 19:1-7, how do we know that the twelve disciples in Ephesus had not received the baptism in the Holy Spirit until Paul laid hands on them?

2. The gift that the disciples in Ephesus received was not tongues, but the gift of the fullness of the Holy Spirit—a gift that enabled them to tell others about Christ. Tongues were the initial evidence (the first outward sign) of that gift. What are your thoughts about speaking in tongues being the sign of the gift, rather than being the actual gift?

3. Paul addressed the twelve disciples as believers: "Did you receive the Holy Spirit when you believed?" What is the significance of Paul recognizing them as believers?

4. John the Baptist had preached about the Holy Spirit (Luke 3:16). So, when Paul asked the twelve disciples about the Holy Spirit, it was not that they were ignorant of the existence of the Spirit's existence. What was it that they did not know?

5. How does Acts 19:1-7 teach us to minister to others who have been saved, but have not yet received the fullness of the Holy Spirit?

Yielding to the Spirit

—Know—

When Paul arrived in Ephesus, he found twelve disciples (Acts 19:1, 7). (In both the Gospel of Luke and the Book of Acts, the writer Luke uses the word "*disciples*" to mean *Christians*.) These disciples were not people who were just interested in, or who were somewhat doubtful about who Jesus was—they were followers of Jesus Christ. Also, they were not simply disciples of John the Baptist, for John the Baptist in his preaching had always called people to repentance and faith in Jesus, the Coming One.

Indications of the outpouring of the Holy Spirit. The outpouring of the Holy Spirit in Jerusalem, Samaria, and on the apostle Paul in Damascus marked not a conversion experience but empowerment for sharing the gospel (Acts 1:8). In Acts 19, the twelve disciples in Ephesus had not yet heard about the outpouring of the Spirit's power that had occurred on the Day of Pentecost. They were followers of Jesus, but had not received the blessing of being filled with the Holy Spirit. That is, they had not yet experienced baptism (immersion) in the Spirit for witnessing. They were filled when Paul laid hands on them. As evidence of that experience, they spoke in tongues and prophesied.

The immediate results of these Ephesian disciples being filled with the Spirit were speaking in tongues and prophesying. Speaking in tongues is a special kind of prophetic, inspired speech and is a fulfillment of "Your sons and your daughters shall prophesy" (Acts 2:17, 18). The correct interpretation is not that some spoke in tongues and others prophesied as a sign of receiving the fullness of the Spirit. But "*and prophesied*" is another way of saying that the disciples spoke in tongues *and gave praise* to God after they received the Pentecostal power of the Spirit (4:4, 11; 10:46; 19:5).

Similarities among accounts in the Bible about the outpouring of the Holy Spirit. By looking at the accounts in the Book of Acts that talk about the Holy Spirit, we can discern a pattern in respect to the initial sign of the baptism in the Spirit. Beginning with Acts 2:4 and reoccurring in 10:46 and 19:6, we see that when believers were filled with the Spirit they spoke in tongues. From these three accounts, Pentecostals have derived their teachings and practice regarding the special blessing of the Holy Spirit, which in the *Declaration of Faith* is referred to as: "*baptism with the Holy Ghost*," and most commonly today is called: "*baptism in the Holy Spirit*."

An understanding in a number of ancient cultures was that three witnesses were needed to establish a truth. Luke's three accounts of tongues accompanying Spirit baptism provide an adequate basis to expect the same manifestation in Spirit baptism today. According to the Book of Acts, this manifestation of the Spirit occurred over a period of twenty years, and took place in various locations: Jerusalem, Caesarea, and the remote area of Ephesus.

—Be—

Having the desire to be filled with the Holy Spirit is to want to receive all the blessings that God has for us. Through Jesus Christ, our heavenly Father gives us the fruit of the Holy Spirit—love, joy, and peace. God also

offers us an additional special blessing from the Spirit—
to empower, comfort, and guide us in witnessing and life.

Although speaking in tongues is the sign that
someone is being baptized in the fullness of the Holy
Spirit, tongues do not bring about this experience. This
blessing of the Spirit is a gift from God for empowered
sharing of the good news about our heavenly Father and
Jesus Christ's love for the world, and for living a
Christlike life.

Consider:

- What blessings do you wish to receive from God
  through the Holy Spirit?

—Do—

As we seek to be open to the move of the Holy Spirit,
it is wise to guard against our passion and focus being
primarily on speaking in tongues. Even though we see
tongues as being the evidence of the Pentecostal
experience, it is best for our attention to be on: a deeper

relationship with the Lord, the fullness of the Holy Spirit, and becoming more effective in the service of God.

As we pray about and focus on a deeper, fuller relationship with God, we can ask God to help us become more open to whatever ways the Spirit may work in our lives—including, speaking in tongues, other manifestations, and spiritual gifts. The Book of Acts discloses that God has given the manifestation of tongues as a sign of the fullness of the Spirit, a sign that occurs at the moment of Spirit baptism. The most important thing is that we trust in God, for God loves us and always knows what is best for us.

Consider:

- What kind of life in the Spirit do you want to live?

Offer a Prayer

Father, I pray now for Your blessing of the fullness of the Holy Spirit. Help me to go deeper in my relationship with You. Help me to receive and live overflowing with the abundance of the Holy Spirit every day of my life— becoming more effective in Your service and welcoming Your miracles. Amen.

Day 5

Corinth

Searching the Scripture

Read Acts 4:31

> *About the friends of Peter and John, who were gathered to*
> *hear them tell about their arrest and release in Jerusalem:*
> And when they had prayed, the place where they were
> assembled together was shaken; and they were all filled
> with the Holy Spirit, and they spoke the word of God with
> boldness.

Read 1 Corinthians 12:7-11

> *From the apostle Paul's letter to the church in Corinth:*
> But the manifestation of the Spirit is given to each one for
> the profit of all: for to one is given the word of wisdom
> through the Spirit, to another the word of knowledge
> through the same Spirit, to another faith by the same
> Spirit, to another gifts of healings by the same Spirit, to

another the working of miracles, to another prophecy, to another discerning of spirits, to another different kinds of tongues, to another the interpretation of tongues. But one and the same Spirit works all these things, distributing to each one individually as He wills.

Answer the Following Questions:

1. According to Acts 4:31, what was an outcome of Jesus' followers being filled with the Spirit?

2. According to 1 Corinthians 12, what are some spiritual gifts that we might observe being used in the life of the church?

3. How would you describe the relationship between *the baptism in the Spirit* and *the gifts of the Spirit* in light of the New Testament? (See "*Know*" section.)

4. What are a few examples of people receiving gifts of the Spirit in the Old Testament? (See "*Know*" section.)

5. What was the pastoral problem that Paul was addressing in 1 Corinthians 12-14?

6. How would you reconcile good order in public worship with the freedom and spontaneity of the Spirit to manifest spiritual gifts?

Yielding to the Spirit

—Know—

The relationship between *baptism in the Spirit* and *gifts of the Spirit*. The mention of *baptism in the Spirit* and *gifts of Spirit* together may make us wonder what the relationship between them is. While *gifts of the Spirit* are the abilities that God gives us to do His work of love, *baptism in the Spirit* is a special blessing of empowerment from the Holy Spirit that helps us to derive Him

In the twentieth century, the Pentecostal revival deepened the conviction of many that: (1) baptism in the Spirit is a Christian experience that follows one's decision to follow Jesus Christ; and (2) God bestows spiritual gifts on believers. This realization motivated many Christians to explore the relationship between baptism in the Spirit and gifts of the Spirit.

Some people have concluded that since spiritual gifts are a *"manifestation of the Spirit"* that baptism in the Spirit must be necessary for receiving gifts of the Spirit. Sometimes, they have described Spirit baptism as being "a gateway" to receiving spiritual gifts. However, Paul points out in his letter to the Corinthian church that: "the manifestation of the Spirit is given *to each one* for the profit of all" (1 Corinthians 12:7). As we consider the meaning of the phrase *"each one"* along with the other issues surrounding spiritual gifts in the church of Corinth, it is helpful to note that many of the gifts that are mentioned in the New Testament also occurred during the Old Testament era.

Spiritual gifts throughout the Bible. Gifts of the Spirit of various types are mentioned in both the Old and New Testaments of the Bible.

Jesus' disciples used spiritual gifts in their ministry with Jesus. Before Pentecost, the day on which the disciples were baptized in (filled with) the Holy Spirit, Jesus sent them to use their spiritual gifts of preaching the gospel, healing the sick, and casting out of demons.

Long before the coming of Christ and the outpouring of the Spirit on the Day of Pentecost, a number of people discussed in the Old Testament had received and used spiritual gifts. The ministries of God's servants during that time were possible because of the special endowments (gifts) of the Holy Spirit.

Some examples of the divine imparting of spiritual gifts to individuals who are discussed in the Old Testament are:

- The gifts of wisdom, knowledge, and craftsmanship were granted to Bezaleel and to those who worked with him on the tabernacle. God instructed Moses to set Bezaleel aside for the work because "I have filled him with the Spirit of God, in wisdom, in understanding, in knowledge, and in all manner of workmanship" (Exodus 31:1-5; compare 35:30-33).

- As Moses successor, Joshua "was full of the spirit of wisdom" (Deuteronomy 34:9).

- In addition to Joshua, the gift of leadership was bestowed on such notable people as Moses, David, and Solomon (Numbers 11:16-17; 1 Samuel 16:13; 1 Kings 3:5-13).

- The gifts of working miracles and healing were prominent in the ministry of Elijah and Elisha (2 Kings 2:6-25; 4:1-5:14).

- The gift of prophecy was much in evidence throughout the Old Testament.

Baptism in the Spirit and openness to God's spiritual gifts. So rather than speaking of baptism in the Spirit as being the *gateway* to receive the gifts of the

Spirit, it is more biblically correct to understand that: God gives at least one spiritual gift to each of us—to each follower of Christ. Also, baptism in/filling with the Spirit helps us to be *more open* to receiving spiritual gifts and *more sensitive* to their operation. After the outpouring of the Spirit, as told in the book of Acts, there was an increase in the gifts of the Spirit such as healings, prophecies, discernment, faith, wisdom, the working of miracles, and the casting out of demons.

This increased openness and sensitivity to the Holy Spirit are why we may observe among Pentecostals freer use of spiritual gifts. More will be said later in *Week Three* about other results of receiving the baptism in the Spirit.

Spiritual gifts in public worship. In 1 Corinthians chapters 12-14, the apostle Paul focuses on a pastoral problem in public worship in the church of Corinth. Apparently, even though many of the people in the Corinthian church were Spirit-filled, they were spiritually immature in their use of the gift of tongues and the gift of prophecy. Paul recognized the unbalanced emphasis that they were placing on these gifts. So, in his letter to the church, he stressed the proper use of the gifts in public worship.

The Corinthians' behavior stood in sharp contrast to God's sacrificial, redemptive love (*agape*). They needed to take a broader view of spiritual gifts and to understand that love was absolutely essential when using any of the gifts. They had become competitive in their use of gifts in public worship.

In chapter 13 of 1 Corinthians, Paul focuses on the Christian virtue of love. Such love should regulate, govern, and control the use of spiritual gifts. As the apostle emphasizes, the "more excellent way" for gifts to operate is through love (1 Corinthians 12:31). In Corinth, the believers had failed to integrate love into their use of the spiritual gifts. Rather than seeking its own, redemptive love constantly seeks what is best for others. The proper operation of the gifts of the Spirit is through love.

—Be—

The gifts of the Spirit working through love truly edify the church and build it up. The opening words of 1 Corinthians 12 reveal that the Corinthian Christians lacked full knowledge of gifts of the Spirit. Some in the Corinthian church, in their pride and failure to love those members of the church who were weaker in their faith, were themselves acting spiritually immature (8:2, 7-13). As Paul saw it, in 1 Corinthians 12, those believers were in danger of being misled by their pride and their faulty misunderstanding of spiritual gifts.

Paul proposes a fundamental test of one's being led by the Spirit: anyone who speaks about Jesus must proclaim Him as Lord (12:3; compare John 16:13-15). When led by the Holy Spirit, a person's words and actions will reflect the love of God. If we are without God's love revealed through the cross and the lordship of Christ, the gifts of the Spirit become tools for glorifying ourselves. Our being open and led by the Spirit will ensure that our worship and the manifestation of spiritual gifts will exalt Jesus Christ.

Consider:

- What spiritual gift(s) have you been given?

- What has been helpful to you in your use of your gift?

- How has using your gift helped you experience God's love in your own life?

- How has using your gift helped you show the love of God to others?

—Do—

A spiritually mature church is a church that consists of individuals who are led by the Spirit and who genuinely exalt Jesus as Lord.

Consider:

What can we in the church do to be in agreement with and to allow the Holy Spirit to use us and our spiritual gifts in mature, loving ways to serve others? Here are some ideas:

- In our public worship, invite the Holy Spirit's presence and allow room for the Spirit to guide and to check what is done during our time of worship (1 Corinthians 12:1-3).
- Remember who the Divine Giver of spiritual gifts is—the Holy Spirit, the "*Spirit of truth*," who knows what is best for us and the church (1 Corinthians 12:7, 11; John 16:13-15).
- Remember that the purpose of spiritual gifts is for the encouragement, building up, and ministry of the church. This includes: (1) every aspect of worship, spiritual growth, and service within the life of the church, as well as (2) the church's outward ministry and invitation to others, which often results in the church's numerical growth (1 Corinthians 14:3-5, 12, 26-33; 1 Peter 4:8-11).
- Learn to live as a body, unified through God's love—for like each member of the human body has its function, so

does each member of the body of Christ (1 Corinthians 12:12-30).

- Know that the gifts of the Spirit are to be manifested in the eternal love of God, which Jesus manifested in His sacrifice on the Cross for the benefit of all (1 Corinthians 13:1-13).
- Practice and encourage order and balance in worship, while making room for freedom and spontaneity, so that the Holy Spirit may manifest His presence and gifts.

After considering these ideas, can you think of ways you want to grow in your use of your own spiritual gift(s)?

Offer a Prayer

Holy Spirit, thank You for Your presence in the life of the church, and for giving each of us spiritual gifts that help us show the love of Christ to each other.

Help me recognize the gift You have given me and to always remember that this gift comes from You. Please teach me to listen to Your guidance. Show me how to grow in my ability to use any spiritual gift You may give me. Amen.

Group Discussion

Key Scripture—Acts 1:8; 2:4

> But you shall receive power when the Holy Spirit has come upon you; and you shall be witnesses to Me in Jerusalem, and in Judea and Samaria, and unto the ends of the earth (Acts 1:8).

> And they were all filled with the Holy Spirit and began to speak with other tongues, as the Spirit gave them the utterance (2:4).

Opening—This is a time of fellowship and sharing about one another's lives.

Prayer

Testimony—Have two or three group members give a testimony of how God is at work in their lives, whether it is through their daily encounters in this study, or some other way.

Discussion Questions:

1. The baptism in the Spirit is a profound experience of the power for telling others about Jesus Christ and living the Christian life. Have a few in the group tell about their baptism in the Spirit and what it means to them.

2. Prepare a definition of *Spirit baptism* (baptism in/of/with the Holy Spirit), and as a group, discuss its significance.

3. Define and discuss *the doctrine of subsequence* in light of the Samaritans' experience of the baptism in the Spirit.

4. Why is it that we believe that Simon saw the Samaritans speaking in tongues after Peter and John prayed for them?

5. The ancient racial-divide of Jews and Gentiles was a fact in the first century. In light of the outpouring of the Spirit on the Gentiles in Caesarea, how should we react to the racial-divide that exists among Christians today?

6. Compare the experience of Jesus being filled with the Spirit at the Jordan River with the filling of the 120 believers on the Day of Pentecost.

7. What is your understanding of the gifts of the Spirit as manifested in the Old Testament and Paul's instructions regarding their use and function in public worship according to 1 Corinthians 12:14?

8. In this week's study about the *Outpouring of the Holy Spirit*, what has impacted you the most?

Closing Prayer

RECEIVING

THE

BAPTISM

OF THE

HOLY SPIRIT

Week 2

Day 1

Faith and Purity of Heart

DECLARATION OF FAITH

"We Believe....

**In the baptism with the Holy Ghost
subsequent to a clean heart."**

Words to Hide in Your Heart

> For I will pour water on him who is thirsty, And floods on the dry ground; I will pour My Spirit on your descendants, And My blessing on your offspring; They will spring up among the grass like willows by the watercourses (Isaiah 44:3-4).

Touching Base

We continue with the distinction between the work of the Holy Spirit in salvation and in Spirit baptism. In the next four days of this study, we will focus on being filled with the Holy Spirit, following salvation. When a person comes to faith in Jesus Christ, that person is in need of instruction, nurture, and mentoring (discipleship) for a life of faith. The full process of this discipleship includes helping a person to welcome and receive the fullness of the Holy Spirit.

Jesus Christ and the Holy Spirit in the life of the church. Pentecostal churches are often very enthusiastic about sharing the good news about Jesus (*evangelism*) and welcoming people into church fellowship (*church growth*). Even so, some churches may fail to follow through on a very important aspect of evangelism and church growth—the equipping of believers (*discipleship*) to live fully in the fruit and empowerment of the Holy Spirit, and to become witnesses for Jesus Christ.

It is good and necessary for the church to be involved in a wide variety of ministry. However, if we are not careful, we may not have the full foundation that we need. We must remember that the church's foundation is Jesus, and that we need help from the Holy Spirit. What is needed in the church is a fervency to develop disciples of Jesus, and to encourage our people to be filled with the Spirit. This is an important responsibility for pastors, local church leaders, and mentors within our congregations. Our leaders need all of us to pray for them.

A deeper dimension of life with the Holy Spirit. The baptism of the Spirit was not only promised to the first believers in the early church, but to followers of Christ today. Clearly, Paul taught that all who come to faith in Jesus Christ are renewed spiritually and indwelt by the Holy Spirit (Romans 8:9), but Peter spoke of a deeper dimension of the Spirit. In fact, on the Day of Pentecost, Peter preached that the outpouring of the Holy Spirit is promised to all who have repented and believed the gospel (Acts 2:33, 39). No believer is excluded.

We can compare baptism in the Spirit to an iceberg. The tip of the iceberg points to a gigantic piece of ice which cannot be seen. Likewise, speaking in tongues can be seen and heard, but the experience of being filled with the Holy Spirit is a much larger spiritual reality than just speaking in tongues. Being filled with the Spirit is a wonderful, empowering experience that intensifies our becoming witnesses for Christ and increases our fervency in devotions and worship.

Now we will learn more about matters that relate to receiving the fullness of the Spirit, such as faith, purity of heart, prayer, obedience, and God's rule and human expectation.

Searching the Scripture

Read Acts 15:8-9:

> So God, who knows the heart, acknowledged them by giving them the Holy Spirit, just as He did to us, and made no distinction between us and them, purifying their hearts by faith.

Answer the Following Questions:

1. In the account in Acts 15:6-12, Peter is talking to the Jerusalem Council (the Jewish religious leaders) about the Gentiles' having been received into the church. He indicates that God accepts everyone, and gives the Holy Spirit to both Jews and non-Jews. The

heavenly Father with the Holy Spirit purifies people's hearts, as they trust and rely on Him.

What is the difference between people relying on the Father, Jesus, and the Holy Spirit (*living in faith*) for purification of their hearts—and people simply following rules (*doing works, living legalistically*) in an attempt to be holy?

2. How might a life of faith help one be more open to the Holy Spirit?

3. After Pentecost, Luke encouraged believers to pray to their heavenly Father for a special anointing of the Spirit (Luke 11:9-13). Why was it that Luke was encouraging believers to seek the Holy Spirit who would produce power and praise in their hearts similar to Jesus (3:21-22) and the early Christians (Acts 2:4; 10:46; 19:6)?

4. In practice, the vital connection between purity of heart and being Spirit-filled is not always maintained. The Corinthian church is an example. It was a Spirit-filled church, but a miserable failure in consistent bearing of the fruit of the Spirit. What are your thoughts regarding this matter in the church today?

Yielding to the Spirit

—Know—

The baptism in the Spirit is a gift from God. Much is said in the Bible about God as the giver of the Spirit. Through our initial faith in Christ, God gives us the Holy Spirit—but as we have noted in our study of the Book of Acts, there is a deeper experience in the Spirit that may be received later. The concern here is the relation of faith and purity of heart to receiving the baptism in the Spirit. God's blessings are received by faith.

The heart purified through faith. Peter spoke about the heart being purified by faith (Acts 15:9). Purifying of the heart (the inward life) is the work of the Holy Spirit in those who have faith in Christ. The Pentecostal gift of the Spirit is for those who are committed through faith in Christ to living a holy life (a life focused on the things of God). To put it another way, the gift of empowerment for witnessing and living can be received by people who have been saved and the Spirit is purifying their hearts.

According to the Book of Acts, this gift of the Holy Spirit was consciously desired and sought by the early Christians (2:4, 4:31; 8:14-15; 19:2). It is important to note that they received the fullness of the Holy Spirit without being perfect.

Preparing our hearts. The heart needs to be prepared for the fullness of the Spirit. This preparation involves faith. Through faith, there has been the forgiveness of sins and the Spirit has renewed the heart. But there may be some debris remaining in one's life, hindering the receiving of the fullness of the Spirit. Some may still struggle with doubt; others may have divided devotion; and still others may have a passionate love of the things of this world.

The early believers needed ten days in Jerusalem before they were filled with the Spirit. Paul, a proud, self-reliant, and bitter Pharisee, was converted from a legalistic religious life to a life of faith in God through Jesus Christ, and was called to ministry. However, he apparently needed more time before he was totally surrendered to the Lord. Three days later in Damascus Saul of Tarsus was filled with the Spirit (Acts 9:9-18).

—*Be*—

From the Day of Pentecost on, God's plan has been to fill all His children with the Spirit (Joel 2:28-29; Acts 2:16-21, 38-39). The baptism in the Spirit is a gift of God, and no matter how hard we may work, no one can earn it. Like salvation, the only way to be filled with the Spirit is by faith. Thank God more and more people are choosing to be participators in the blessings that God has for them through the Holy Spirit.

Consider:

- How open are you to the blessings of the Holy Spirit?

- Do you have any reservations or questions about receiving and living in the fullness of the Spirit?

- Is there anything hindering your putting your trust in God and receiving the blessing of the fullness of the Spirit?

—Do—

Faith is not a work. What are we to do as believers? We should be open and sensitive to whatever God may lead us to do. That involves placing ourselves in the hands of God who delights in giving His children the empowerment of the Spirit to live a holy life of love. God must be allowed to remove whatever may be hindering us from receiving the blessing of the Spirit's power. As we will see, it is by faith, particularly demonstrated by prayer, obedience, and expectancy, that the Pentecostal gift is received.

Offer a Prayer

Lord Jesus, thank You for Your saving grace. Help me to trust You and to live a life of faith, rather than trying to make it on my own. Purify my heart, and help me release my attachment to things that are not Your will for me. May I always be receptive to the fullness of Holy Spirit. Amen.

Day 2

Receiving the Baptism
of the Spirit:
Prayer

Searching the Scripture

Read Acts 1:13-14:

> And when they had entered, they went up into the upper
> room where they were staying: Peter, James, John, and
> Andrew; Philip and Thomas; Bartholomew and Matthew;
> James the son of Alphaeus and Simon the Zealot; and
> Judas the son of James. These all continued with one
> accord in prayer and supplication, with the women and
> Mary the mother of Jesus, and with His brothers.

Answer the Following Questions:

1. What were the men and women who were gathered
   in an upper room in Jerusalem on the Day of

Pentecost doing when "they were all filled with the Holy Spirit"? (Acts 1:1-14; 2:1-4).

2. Acts 1:14 states "these all continued with one accord in prayer and supplication." These disciples, followers of Jesus, were united in their commitment to prayer and their purpose for being there. The word "*supplication*" in this verse indicates that they were requesting something from God. What did they seek?

3. Can you list some occasions in the Bible in which prayer was the background for people being filled with the Spirit? (See "*Know*" section.)

4.   How do we know from Acts chapter 1 that when the 120 disciples came to Jerusalem, they were Christians?

Yielding to the Spirit

—Know—

Devotion to prayer and the Spirit's blessings. Receiving baptism in the Holy Spirit is closely connected to prayer. When Jesus was filled with the Spirit, He was praying (Luke 3:21-22). In Jerusalem before the Day of Pentecost, the disciples were devoting themselves to prayer until the Spirit came on them (Acts 1:13-14).

Other people whose stories are recorded in the New Testament also devoted themselves to prayer. For example, Peter and John prayed before the Samaritans received the fullness of the Spirit (8:14-15). In a vision, the Lord told Ananias to go to the house where Saul might be found, "for behold, he [Saul] is praying" (9:10-11).

Ananias, who ministered to Saul, prayed for him to receive his sight and to "be filled with the Holy Spirit" (9:17). Later, in chapter 10 of Acts, prayer was in the background of Cornelius and his friends being filled with the Spirit (10:2, 4, 9). In fact, prayer was offered from both sides—Peter who would minister and Cornelius who would receive the Spirit.

Persistence in prayer and God's timing. Jesus emphasized the importance of persistence in prayer: ask . . . seek . . . knock (Luke 11:9). As a climax, He adds, "If you then, being evil, know how to give good gifts to your children, how much more will your heavenly Father give the Holy Spirit to those who ask Him!"(v.13). Ernest and sincere prayer to the Father is a vital means of receiving the blessed gift. Soon after Peter began to preach to Cornelius and his friends, their sins were forgiven and hearts renewed. Those devout people were ready for the mighty anointing of the Holy Spirit.

At times, the Spirit may be immediately poured out without an extended time of prayer. After Jesus was baptized and while He was praying, the Holy Spirit descended on Him. Prayer invites God's holy presence and prepares the atmosphere in which God delights to baptize believers in the Spirit. Frequently in the midst of prayer, the Holy Spirit has been received.

The Holy Spirit and mission. Jesus told His disciples that it was not for them to know when the kingdom of God would come in its fullness. He did not want them to worry about it, but He wanted them to get their priorities right. The priority was "you shall be witnesses to Me" (Acts 1:8). "You shall be" means "sharing the love of Jesus with others is not optional—but is to be an integral part of who we are as followers of Christ in the inspiration and empowerment of the Holy Spirit." There is a strong missional connection to being baptized in the Spirit. In the history of the church, missions and evangelistic work—at home and abroad—greatly expanded when believers realized they were dependent on the power of the Holy Spirit.

The Holy Spirit empowers us to bear witness in two ways: The first way is a matter of lifestyle in which the Holy Spirit empowers us to live a Christlike life and show love in practical ways. The Holy Spirit gives us ample opportunities and power to do things that allow God's light to shine in our lives. The second way is the spoken word in which the Holy Spirit empowers us to teach, to preach, to witness, and to give personal testimonies. God works in these many ways to reach others with the gospel.

—Be—

Soon after the disciples were filled with the Spirit on the Day of Pentecost, they were confronted by opposition and hostility. They prayed for boldness to minister in the name of Jesus (Acts 4:29-30). God answered their prayers by granting a fresh filling of the Spirit (v. 31). Regardless of circumstances, we need to be people totally devoted to the service of Christ. When our lives are in God's hands and we desire to be used of God, the power of the Holy Spirit abounds through us to the glory of God.

Consider:

- What impact do you think persistence in prayer has on our being filled with the Holy Spirit?

- Many people who have been filled with the Spirit share that when they had that experience, they were praying and praising God. What have been your experiences with the Holy Spirit?

—*Do*—

The profound experience of Spirit baptism is for all believers. When people hear that statement or a similar one, they may ask, "*What must we do to be filled with the Spirit?*" The answer is that it is not so much a matter of *doing* as it is *being* a believer and having a genuine desire to be filled with the Spirit.

Our pioneers in the Pentecostal Movement, in seeking the baptism in the Spirit, knew the importance of prayer. They were unwilling to settle for anything less than a Pentecostal encounter with the Holy Spirit. On occasions they "tarried" and engaged in prayer for long periods of time in order to focus on God and to become more receptive to the Holy Spirit's work in their lives. They realized that it takes time and effort to move from being focused on oneself to being truly focused on God, hearing His voice and submitting one's life to Him.

Consider:

- What do you think about making more time in worship services for prayer and seeking the Holy Spirit?

- How do you think that would impact the spiritual life of the church and its mission?

Offer a Prayer

Holy Spirit, You help us pray, and through our prayers, You empower us. Please help me set aside time to pray and to listen to God. Help me to wait with an open heart for all that You have for me. In Jesus' name, I pray. Amen.

Day 3

Obedience

Read Acts 5:29-32:

Peter addressing the Sanhedrin (the supreme council and court of justice of the Jews):

> But Peter and the other apostles answered and said: "We ought to obey God rather than men. The God of our fathers raised up Jesus whom you murdered by hanging on a tree. Him God has exalted to His right hand to be Prince and Savior, to give repentance to Israel and forgiveness of sins. And we are His witnesses to these things, and so also is the Holy Spirit whom God has given to those who obey Him."

Answer the Following Questions:

1. In Acts 5:29, what do you think Peter means when he says, "We ought to obey God rather than men"?

2. On the basis of Scripture, what would you tell a person who is seeking to be filled with the Spirit about personal obedience? (See "*Know*" section below.) Do you have a favorite Bible promise regarding the gift of the Spirit?

3. Obedience lies at the heart of faith. Since the Holy Spirit is the Spirit of holiness, why would a person's intention and direction to obey the word of the Lord be important to placing him or her in the position to be filled with the Spirit?

Yielding to the Spirit

—*Know*—

The disciples' obedience. Before Christ ascended into heaven, He promised His disciples that they would be baptized in the Holy Spirit. This promise depended on their obedience to His command to wait in Jerusalem for the outpouring of the Holy Spirit. This blessing was God's provision, but the command of Jesus established obedience through faith as necessary for the receiving of the gift. The disciples obeyed Jesus' command: "Tarry in the city of Jerusalem until you are endued with power from on high" (Luke 24:49). Their obedience sprang from faith in God, and they were filled with the Spirit (Acts 1:4).

Saul's obedience. Similarly, to the disciples, Saul of Tarsus obeyed Jesus' instructions. Saul asked, "Lord, what do You want me to do?" The Lord told him, "Arise and go into the city, and you will be told what you must do (Acts 9:6). After Saul arrived in Damascus, Ananias received a command: "Arise and go to the street called Straight and inquire at the house of Judas for one called Saul of Tarsus . . . (v. 11). The obedience of both Saul and Ananias resulted in Saul receiving the Pentecostal gift of the Spirit (v. 17).

Jesus' instructions. The words of Jesus: "*Ask . . . seek . . . knock . . .*" are a strong threefold command (Luke 11:9-11). This command is related to receiving the Holy Spirit. We should not assume that it is necessary to have a direct command from Jesus. Whether we have a direct word from Him (as did Saul and the disciples) or not, what is important is putting our trust in Jesus and obeying Him. We can do this by living in agreement with Jesus' words and the way He lived His life on this earth.

Obedience and the Holy Spirit. Peter connected obedience to receiving of the Spirit. In Acts 5, Peter begins his speech before the Sanhedrin with the words: "We ought to obey God rather than men" (v. 29) and he ends it with "And we are His witnesses to these things, and so also is the Holy Spirit whom God has given to those who obey Him" (v. 32). The Sanhedrin did not have the Holy Spirit because they did not obey God.

Obedience and the heart. Obedience is the proper attitude of heart and will, as the words of Jesus indicate in John's Gospel: "If you love Me, keep My commandments. And I will pray the Father, and He will give you another Helper, that He may abide with you forever— the Spirit of truth" (John 14:15-16). Like the disciples, we can do the work of Jesus because He went to the Father and sent the Holy Spirit to empower us. All three members of the Trinity are mentioned here. They work together, giving abundant blessings, in response to the obedience of God's people.

Obedience does not call for perfection, but for us to be devoted to doing the will of God.

—Be—

Obedience is a profound expression of faith in God and His promises. This involves accepting Jesus as Lord as well as Savior. The Book of Acts emphasizes yielding and being obedient to the Lord. The climax to the 120 disciples' prayers and obeying the Lord was the outpouring of the Spirit.

Paul's experience was similar. He had been a proud and self-reliant man who, in his efforts to be obedient, was having Christians thrown in prison and was trying to destroy the church (Galatians 1:13-14). Christ's encounter with Him on the road to Damascus redirected his life, and his understanding of obedience to God. The three days He spent in blindness, prayer, and fasting enabled him to more and more to yield himself to the Lord, to God's grace, and to be filled with the Spirit (Acts 9:15-19). Devoted obedience to the Lord is an expression of strong faith and is vital to receiving the fullness of the Spirit.

Consider:

- How has this lesson about obedience, changed the way you think about baptism in the Holy Spirit?
- What do you think being obedient to God (living according to His law of love and becoming prayerful and open to His blessings and guidance) would mean for your life?

—Do—

Obedience and God's Word. It is necessary for leaders in the Christian church and all followers of Jesus Christ to be attentive and obedient to the teachings of God's Word. If we take a fresh look at the Scriptures, and also carefully examine our statements of faith, both of these can greatly impact how we live our lives.

Obedience and gifts of the Spirit. At the heart of missionary service and many people coming to know the love of Jesus, has been the Pentecostal emphasis on the gifts of the Spirit in corporate worship. As the church has told about and reflected (in its worship and life) the graciousness of Jesus and the empowerment of the Spirit—millions and millions of people have come to believe in Jesus and to receive a life-changing, empowering experience in the Holy Spirit.

Consider:

- How might we in our fellowships be more obedient to God, and invite the presence of the Holy Spirit?

- How might we help regular worship participants and visitors understand and feel more comfortable with manifestations of the Spirit?

Offer a Prayer

Jesus, thank You for coming to this earth to teach and to show us how to be obedient to Your way of love. Today, I pray, teach me to love as You loved. Help me in obedience to welcome the blessings and guidance of the Holy Spirit. Amen.

Day 4
Yielding

Searching the Scripture

Read Acts 1:12-14

> Then they returned to Jerusalem from the mount called Olivet, which is near Jerusalem, a Sabbath day's journey. And when they had entered, they went up into the upper room where they were staying: Peter, James, John, and Andrew; Philip and Thomas; Bartholomew and Matthew; James the son of Alphaeus and Simon the Zealot; and Judas the son of James. [14] These all continued with one accord in prayer and supplication, with the women and Mary the mother of Jesus, and with His brothers.

Answer the Following Questions:

1. In Acts chapter 1, what indication is there that the disciples were yielding to God?

2. What did the phrase "*one accord*" mean in reference to the 120 disciples staying in the upper room?

3. Why do you think Paul spent three days in Damascus after his conversion in prayer and yielding himself to the Lord? (See "*Know*" section below.)

4. Why should blessings from being filled with the Holy Spirit not overshadow what God has done for us in saving and sanctifying us?

Yielding to the Spirit

—Know—

The disciples' yielding to the Holy Spirit. Jesus had promised His disciples help and power for taking the gospel to the ends of the earth:

- The Holy Spirit had anointed Jesus for ministry, the same ministry to which His disciples and we are called—to show compassion and to share the Good News (the gospel) (Luke 4:18-19).

- Jesus told His disciples to share the Good News with all peoples and nations (Matthew 28:16-20).

- Jesus promised the disciples that the Father would give them a Helper, the Spirit of truth (John 14:16-17).

- Jesus instructed His disciples to pray and wait for the promised Holy Spirit, who would give them "power from on high" (Luke 24:49).

In Acts 1:12-14, on a Sabbath the followers of Jesus went to an upper room to pray and wait on the Holy Spirit. They waited there steadfastly, totally yielding themselves to God. Just prior to Pentecost, these disciples spent about ten days in that room. No doubt, much of that time was devoted to prayer and yielding themselves to God.

As the book of Acts tells us, they were there in "one accord," which literally means of the same mind. This did not mean they all had the same thoughts and feelings about everything, but it did mean that they were united together in yielding to God and waiting to be filled with the power of the Spirit, which Jesus had promised. The climax of Jesus' disciples yielding themselves more and more to God was the outpouring of the Spirit.

The apostle Paul's yielding to the Holy Spirit. The book of Acts emphasizes the importance of being totally devoted to God. In the life of Paul, we have another example of this yielding devotion. Paul's encounter with the living Christ on the road to Damascus transformed him and set him on a new course.

After Paul made his decision to follow Jesus Christ and answer Jesus' call to ministry, he experienced three days of blindness, fasting, and prayer. Yet he must have needed to be much more yielded to the Lord. Most likely during this time, Paul became more fully yielded to his Savior, for when Ananias laid his hands upon him, Paul was filled with the Holy Spirit. Ananias said "'Brother Saul, the Lord Jesus, who appeared to you on the road as you came, has sent me that you may receive your sight and be filled with the Holy Spirit.' Immediately there fell from his eyes something like scales, and he received his sight at once; and he arose and was baptized" (Acts 9:17-18).

Saul's later ministry clearly showed that he had been filled with the Spirit. Inspired by the Holy Spirit, he became more and more powerful in his preaching (vs. 19-22).

A definition of *yielding.* Yielding ourselves to the Lord Jesus Christ means that we truly accept Christ as our *Lord*—the Master/Ruler of our lives, and accept Him as our *Savior*—the One who saves and delivers us from darkness and gives us life. The Scriptures summon us to fully surrender to Him.

When we put away selfishness, renounce personal pride, and totally commit to the Lord, we become more open to receiving the Pentecostal anointing of the Spirit. On the Day of Pentecost, the disciples in the upper room had a hunger and thirst for the power of the Spirit that Christ had promised them. They had prepared their hearts and minds by yielding themselves to the Lord so that they would receive the baptism in the Spirit.

Yielding to the blessings of salvation, sanctification, and baptism in the Holy Spirit. Being filled with the Spirit is a blessed experience. It has a dynamic influence on our total existence in Christ—giving us a profound sense of God's presence, inspiring a greater boldness in witnessing, and enriching our relationship with other people. The results are extraordinary, but none of the results should diminish the importance of what God has done for us in: *saving us* (delivering and giving us freedom to live forever in His love, joy, and peace, as His children and heirs) and *sanctifying us* (cleansing and healing our hearts and lives, and placing us in right, good standing with Him).

—Be—

Every Christian should have a strong desire to be filled with the Holy Spirit. Being convinced that the fullness of the Spirit is vital to the Christian life is an important dimension of yielding to the Spirit.

It is also important for us to realize that there is a difference in *the indwelling of the Holy Spirit* (the Spirit's coming to dwell in us when we commit our lives to Jesus) and our experiencing *the Holy Spirit's fullness*. This understanding will inspire us to become totally yielded to the Lord and receptive to all the blessings that He has for us. *Yielding* creates in us an openness to receiving the fullness of the Spirit.

As we give our lives to God and endeavor to live in a Christ-like way, our first priority must be to become fully yielded to the Lord. In so doing, we will be able to walk daily in the fruit of the Spirit and to experience the richness of the Holy Spirit's blessings in our lives.

Consider:

- Are there areas of your heart that you would like to entrust and yield to God (your Divine Father, Savior Jesus, and Holy Spirit)?

- What might this expanded trust and yielding mean for your spiritual life?

—*Do*—

It is God through Jesus Christ who saves us and provides us abundant eternal life. We cannot save ourselves. Both salvation and the fullness of the Spirit require human cooperation and yielding—graciously made possibly by the Holy Spirit.

To become fully yielded to the Lord, the following is essential:

- *Salvation.* Come to Jesus, accepting the love, forgiveness, life, and blessings He wants to give you—that is, the salvation He offers you. Give Him your life, and rest in the fact that you can trust Him with all of your life, including your future.

- *Baptism in the Spirit.* Like salvation, know that baptism in the Spirit is free. This blessing is as Peter described it when he was speaking about the Gentiles: "God gave them the same gift as He gave us [on the Day of Pentecost] when we believed on the Lord Jesus Christ (Acts 11:17a).

- *Prayer with other Christians.* Engage in prayer with spiritual brothers and sisters who can assist you in being fully yielded to the Lord and open to the move Spirit. The Bible advises us to draw strength and encouragement from our Christian family.

- *Dedication to prayer.* Persist in prayer, asking for the fullness of the Spirit. In his gospel, Luke urged believers to pray for the Pentecostal anointing of the Holy Spirit when he said, "keep on asking…keep on seeking…keep on knocking" (Luke 11:9, NLT).

Consider:

- Are there actions that you want to take to help you yield more fully to God's will and the blessings that He has for you?

- Do you think that Spirit-filled brothers and sisters can assist you in yielding to the Lord and receiving the fullness of the Spirit?

- What might walking in the fullness of the Holy Spirit mean for your daily life?

Offer a Prayer

Lord Jesus, please teach me to yield to God and to be receptive to the Holy Spirit's presence in my life.

Holy Spirit, fill me with Your presence, so that I may wisely, compassionately, and enthusiastically serve and share with others the Good News about Jesus and His love for them. Amen.

Day 5

God's Rule and Human Expectation

Searching the Scripture

Read Acts 1:4-5:

> And being assembled together with them [the apostles], He [Jesus] commanded them not to depart from Jerusalem, but to wait for the Promise of the Father, "which," He said, "you have heard from Me; for John truly baptized with water, but you shall be baptized with the Holy Spirit not many days from now."

Answer the Following Questions:

1. What does Jesus' command to His followers to go to Jerusalem and wait for the promised Holy Spirit, indicate to us about God's rule? What does it indicate to us about the expectation that Jesus' followers had? (See Acts 1:4-5.)

2. What do you think about Peter's declaration that the outpouring of the Spirit was not a one-time event? (See Acts 2:39.)

3. How would you explain the relation of the sovereign rule of God and the baptism in the Spirit? (See "*Know*" section.)

Yielding to the Spirit

—*Know*—

We have emphasized that faith is important in receiving the baptism in the Spirit, and from faith springs purity of heart, prayer, and obedience. Now, we will look at *God's rule and human expectation.* We must not overlook that God is the sovereign Lord, meaning that He is free to fill those who believe with the Holy Spirit when He wills.

God's sovereignty. On the divine side, God rules as Lord. Even so, all things that occur must not be considered to be the direct will of God—for on the human side, His reign always allows for human freedom. Also, in this world, there exists sin and darkness, which affects us all. Obviously, some actions and events do not please God or bring Him glory. In God's plan of mercy and grace, He makes room for our freedom and our coming short of being perfect.

Even with our personal shortcomings and the tragic events and circumstances of this world, God accomplishes His plan for the gospel (which is to bring about faith and true life through Jesus Christ). This plan of love gives Him "good pleasure" (pleases Him) and shows His "glory" (Luke 12:32). In the freedom God gives us, faith is a critical matter. It is important for us to continue to believe and trust in God's will for us and His timing.

Outpouring of the Spirit in the Last Days. Many of us firmly believe that we are living in the last chapter of "the last days." There is little doubt that we are living in extraordinary times in which the Holy Spirit is being poured out. God has promised that in the last days He would pour out the Spirit on all flesh. If we are living in the last chapter of this period of time on earth, what we are witnessing is God's sovereign work in sending the Holy Spirit. When God sends the Holy Spirit, it is primarily a matter of His will and purpose in fulfilling His promise.

On the Day of Pentecost, Peter said to the multitude, "The promise is to you and to your children, and to all who are afar off, as many as the Lord our God will call" (Acts 2:39). The fulfillment of the promise was not exhausted in Peter's day. The words "afar off" reaffirm God's promise to pour out the Spirit on "all flesh" (Acts 2:17) and on people in all places and generations. Throughout the world, there has been an outpouring of the Spirit in our day. Very possibly this could be in preparation for the second coming of Christ.

Human expectancy. Let us not forget the importance of the human expectancy. The 120 at Pentecost expected the outpouring of the Spirit. As believers, they were steadfast in prayer and obedience anticipating the promise of God. Christ had kindled their expectations by telling them to wait in Jerusalem for the Father's promise. Their response was an intense and confident expectation, but they did not know exactly when the promise would be fulfilled.

No doubt Peter' s promise built great expectation among the early believers, but the baptism of the Spirit was not just for them in that time. Everyone who calls on the Lord stands under the same promise.

—*Be*—

Knowing that God is the "only Potentate, the King of kings and Lords of lords," gives us the assurance that God is all powerful and able to keep His promises (1 Timothy 6:15). There is nothing too hard for Him (Jeremiah 32:17-23) and all things are possible with Him (Mark 10:27). Just the thought of God's rule should be an occasion for our praise and obedience and should inspire our expectation that He will baptize believers in the Holy Spirit.

Initial faith in Christ brings us salvation, but we need to continue to believe in seeking the baptism in the Spirit and living the Christian life. With our hearts prepared by the Holy Spirit and our deep commitment to the Lord, we can be ready to receive the Pentecostal experience.

Consider:

- To help you be ready and expectant to receive the outpouring of the blessings of the Holy Spirit, what do you need from God?

- Do you want God's help in changing any expectations?

—*Do*—

The basic condition for receiving the Pentecostal experience is faith. Walking in faith gives rise to purity of heart, prayer, obedience, and expectation of God doing mighty things. These are essential to the Christian life and are vital to the receiving of this gift of the Spirit.

In living the Christian life, the believer needs to consciously and earnestly seek the baptism in the Spirit. In fact, Spirit baptism should not be regarded as a gift that is automatically bestowed on the believer. According to the Book of Acts, this gift was desired and sought after, then received by the early Christians (1:4, 14; 4:31; 8:14-15; 19:2). God gives the baptism to those who earnestly desire it—to those who "ask . . . seek . . . knock" (Luke 11:9-13).

Consider:

- To help you be ready and expectant to receive the outpouring of the blessings of the Holy Spirit, what do you think you need to do?

- What are some ways you can help those who are seeking to be filled with the Spirit to build expectant faith?

Offer a Prayer

Sovereign Lord, give me an expectant heart to receive the outpouring of the Holy Spirit. Help me also to be an encouragement to others in their faith, letting them know that You want to bless each of us with Your promised gift of the Holy Spirit. Amen.

Group Discussion

Key Scripture—Isaiah 44:3-4

> For I will pour water on him who is thirsty, and floods on the dry ground; I will pour My Spirit on your descendants, and My blessing on your offspring; they will spring up among the grass like willows by the watercourses (Isaiah 44:3-4).

Opening—This is a time of fellowship and sharing about one another's lives.

Prayer

Testimony—Have two or three group members give a testimony of how God is at work in their lives, whether it is through their daily encounters in this study, or some other way.

Discussion Questions:

1. Explain the vital connection between purity of heart and being filled with Spirit. How should the failure of the Corinthian Church in this regard be viewed by Spirit-filled believers?

2. Prayer was important to the early Christians in receiving the baptism in the Spirit. Both the believers at Pentecost and the devout Gentile Cornelius in Caesarea were ready to receive the fullness of the Spirit. How vital was prayer to you in receiving this experience? What place does prayer have in living in the fullness of the Spirit?

3. What is the importance of obedience in receiving Spirit baptism?

4. Why do you think that both the 120 followers of Christ at Pentecost and Paul after his conversion spent time in prayer and yielding themselves to the Lord before they were filled with the Spirit?

5. What is the relation between God's rule and human expectancy in receiving the baptism in the Spirit?

6. Sum up what the Scriptures teach about the experience of being filled with Spirit.

7. In this week's study about *Receiving the Baptism in the Holy Spirit* what has impacted you the most?

Closing Prayer

RESULTS

OF BEING

BAPTIZED

IN THE

HOLY SPIRIT

Week 3

Day 1

Divine Enablement for Service

DECLARATION OF FAITH

"*We Believe....*

In the baptism with the Holy Ghost subsequent to a clean heart."

"*We Believe....*

In speaking with other tongues as the Spirit gives utterance and that it is the initial evidence of the baptism of the Holy Ghost."

Words to Hide in Your Heart

And it shall come to pass in the last days, says God, "That I will pour out of My Spirit on all flesh; your sons and your daughters shall prophesy, your young men shall see visions, your old men shall dream dreams. And on My menservants and on My maidservants I will pour out My Spirit in those days; and they shall prophesy" (Acts 2:17-18).

Touching Base

A brief review of articles eight and nine of the Declaration of Faith:

The *baptism of the Holy Spirit* first took place at Pentecost. On that occasion, the disciples were baptized in/filled with the Spirit. Their experience was accompanied by a sound from heaven, tongues like as fire, and *speaking in tongues* (Acts 2:1-4).

Speaking in tongues. Speaking in tongues was also the continuing sign (initial evidence) of the later outpourings of the Spirit in the Book of Acts (10:44-46; 19:1-7). Just as audible, visible signs accompanied Jesus' filling with the Spirit at the Jordon River (Luke 3:22), the Spirit baptism of the disciples was revealed by the manifestation of tongues. On the Day of Pentecost, Peter spoke of the experience that the crowd could both "see and hear" (Acts 2:33).

The Scripture teaches that the baptism in the Spirit is distinct, occurring after a person decides to follow Jesus Christ. In the *Declaration of Faith*, the idea of tongues as being "*initial evidence*" emphasizes that the infilling of the Spirit has been experienced. The term "*tongues*" refers to the immediate, physical effect on the person filled with the Spirit. On the other hand, the word "*evidence*" points to tongues as being the sign of spiritual empowerment and anointing that is received after conversion. The experience of speaking in tongues is in tongues or languages unknown by the speaker.

Other aspects of being filled with the Holy Spirit. The initial manifestation of the presence and power of the Holy Spirit is not the whole picture. In addition to the initial evidence, the Scriptures speak about continuing and internal evidences of Spirit baptism. Among them is personal commitment to witnessing, the teachings of the Bible, and Christian fellowship and worship. As we explore the results of baptism in the Spirit, we will look at these in more detail.

Just a reminder—Spirit baptism is for all who have been saved. Peter promised that the Pentecostal gift is for all future generations. It is an intense spiritual experience that will continue to be available to all genuine believers until the return of Jesus Christ (Acts 2:38-39).

This week we will consider the results of the baptism in the Spirit: (1) Divine Enablement for Service, (2) Greater Spiritual Sensitivity and Openness to Gifts of the Spirit, (3) Greater Consecration and Love of God, and (4) Greater Joy.

Searching the Scripture

Read Luke 24:49 and Acts 1:8:

Jesus speaking to the apostles:

Luke 24:49:
"Behold, I send the Promise of My Father upon you; but tarry in the city of Jerusalem until you are endued with power from on high."

Acts 1:8:
"But you shall receive power when the Holy Spirit has come upon you; and you shall be witnesses to Me in Jerusalem, and in all Judea and Samaria, and to the end of the earth."

Answer the Following Questions:

1. In Luke 24:49 and Acts 1:8, Jesus was talking to His disciples about the Holy Spirit. What did Jesus

indicate that this Promise of His Father would give them?

2. What are some examples in the Book of Acts where it is stated that the Word of God increased and the church continued to grow?

3. Why were signs, wonders and miracles vital in the evangelistic outreach of the early church?

4. The results of being baptized in the Spirit are great, but the blessings of this experience do not diminish the great blessings of salvation and sanctification. Why is this true?

Yielding to the Spirit

—Know—

Many promises are given in the Bible, but "the Promise of the Father" relates to the outpouring of the Spirit (Luke 24:49; Acts 1:4). The Book of Acts and the modern Pentecostal Movement bear witness to the fulfillment of the Father's promise and its powerful results.

From the view of the Bible, power for Christian service is one of the major results of being filled with the Spirit. According to Acts 1:8, "You shall receive power (*dunamis)* when the Holy Spirit has come upon you." This promise was echoed earlier in Jesus' words, instructing His disciples to stay in Jerusalem until they were "endued with power from on high" (Luke 24:49). The disciples could not accomplish the mission that the Lord gave them without the enabling power of the Holy Spirit.

Jesus' empowerment from the Spirit. Jesus himself was an example of this empowerment. From the start of His ministry, the Holy Spirit equipped Him with power. Jesus was "filled with the Holy Spirit" (Luke 4:1). After the wilderness temptation, "Jesus returned in the power of the Spirit to Galilee (v. 14). The Savior intended for His people to have the same powerful anointing for service. When the Spirit was poured out at Pentecost and thereafter, those believers received more than mere strength or ability; they received dynamic power for service.

Spiritual empowerment for mission. The baptism in the Spirit enabled them to be effective servants of God and it does the same for us. This is seen in three ways:

(1) *Power for witnessing.* After Peter was filled with the Spirit, he gave a powerful testimony about Jesus Christ (Acts 2:22-36). The Holy Spirit brought conviction of sin, repentance, and forgiveness, and led three thousand people to salvation (vv. 37, 38, 41). A number of times, we are told in the Book of Acts that the word increased and that the church continued to grow (6:7; 9:31; 12:24; 16:5; 19:20; 28:30-31).

(2) *Power for doing mighty works.* Again and again by the power of the Holy Spirit, Jesus performed miracles and did mighty works. Following the wilderness temptation, not only did Jesus do powerful preaching and teaching but also He was "healing all kinds of sickness and all kinds of disease among the people" (Matthew 4:23; compare Luke 5:24). It was not uncommon for Jesus to cast out demons "by the Spirit of

God" (Matthew 12:28; Mark 16:17-18; Luke 9:1-2; 10:17).

After Jesus' ascension into heaven, the disciples did mighty works—signs, wonders, and miracles. The baptism in the Spirit enabled them to do these works and to cast out demons (Acts 19:11-12). Stephen also was anointed by the Spirit to cast out demons and to heal many who were paralyzed and lame (Acts 6:5, 8). Many others did miraculous works by the power of the Spirit.

(3) *Power to withstand opposition and persecution.* The early Christians were strong in Pentecostal power, but they lived in a world that was hostile to the gospel (hostile to the message that Jesus was the Messiah sent by God). Bearing witness to Jesus did not always prompt a positive response from unbelievers. Although the gospel at times aroused opposition, bearing witness to it was still effective (Acts 9:20-25). Before the outpouring of the Spirit at Pentecost, all the Lord's disciples had forsaken Him (Matthew 26:56; Mark 14:50), but Peter went so far as to deny any knowledge of Him (Matthew 26:69-75). But after they received the power of the Spirit, Jesus' disciples became people with great courage. Their new-found courage can only be explained as the result of their being filled with the Spirit (Acts 2:36; 4:13; 4:28-31; 7:51; 9:17-20).

Articles Eight and Nine

—Be—

Christians are to bear witness to Christ regardless of the response. For the early Christians, the baptism in the Spirit did not become merely a past experience, but it was a dynamic, ongoing reality. That reality enabled them to remain steadfast in the face of hostility and persecution, and to remain faithful to their Lord. The fullness of the Spirit made a remarkable difference in their lives and should do likewise in our lives. The experience helps us to walk and live in the Spirit, which strengthens our commitment to holy living and gives us a greater desire to please Christ.

Consider:

- As a representative of Jesus Christ, have you ever experienced opposition, discrimination, or persecution? If so, consider if during those times, the Holy Spirit was giving you strength and courage.

—*Do*—

Spirit baptism equips believers to be powerful witnesses for the Lord. Signs, miracles and healings confirm the message of the gospel. The New Testament teaches us that the powerful witness to God's Word, accompanied by miracles and healings, are to continue until Christ returns. Mark 16 says, "These signs will follow those who believe." Among the signs listed are the casting out of demons, speaking in new tongues, and the healing of the sick (vv. 17-18).

Healings and other miracles did not cease with the death of the last of the Twelve Apostles. Miraculous signs reach to the present day and beyond to the second coming of Christ. During biblical times, signs ministered to the needs of people, and they still do.

Empowered by the Spirit, the early believers "continued steadfastly in the apostles' doctrine and fellowship, in the breaking of bread, and in prayers" (Acts 2:42). They were keenly aware of the Holy Spirit in their daily lives, and they went about with an intense desire to yield to the guidance of the Spirit. The actions of Spirit-filled Christians today should be no different. The Holy Spirit is still the Spirit of love, fellowship, holiness, and mighty works.

Offer a Prayer

Holy Spirit, thank You for the help and empowerment You give us to do the work of the Lord. I pray now for wisdom, courage, ability, and strength so that I can be faithful in serving, and telling others the good news. Amen.

Day 2

Greater Spiritual Sensitivity and Openness to Gifts of the Spirit

Searching the Scripture

Read John 16:13-15:

> However, when He, the Spirit of truth, has come, He will guide you into all truth; for He will not speak on His own authority, but whatever He hears He will speak; and He will tell you things to come. He will glorify Me, for He will take of what is Mine and declare it to you. All things that the Father has are Mine. Therefore I said that He will take of Mine and declare it to you.

Answer the Following Questions:

1. According to John 16:13-15, on whose authority does the Holy Spirit speak and act? Whom does the Holy Spirit glorify in all that He does?   Jesus

2. In verse 15, Jesus says, "He will take of Mine and declare [make known] it to you." How might this promise relate to gifts of the Holy Spirit?

3. What are some examples in the Old Testament of people using gifts of the Holy Spirit? Also, some examples in the New Testament?

Yielding to the Spirit

—Know—

Spiritual sensitivity. The experience of the disciples on the Day of Pentecost gave them a deeper spiritual understanding and increased their openness to the Spirit. As well as giving believers power for witnessing and service, the Holy Spirit came to lead them into spiritual truth. According to Jesus, "When He, the Spirit of truth, has come, He will guide you into all [spiritual] truth" (John 16:13). The truth that the Spirit brings is found in Jesus Christ. The Spirit takes the things of Christ and makes them known to believers (16:13-16).

Filled with the Spirit, Peter was enlightened and inspired to preach the gospel. Stephen was described as a man "full of the Holy Spirit and wisdom" (Acts 6:3). He spoke so forcefully that his opponents could not "resist the wisdom and the Spirit by which he spoke" (v. 10). The message that he preached clearly showed that He had a grasp of the biblical truth (7:2-53).

Openness to the gifts of the Spirit. The anointing of the Spirit gave the early Christians a grasp of the gospel, but also it enabled them to be more open to the gifts of the Spirit. Pentecostals link very closely Spirit baptism and the gifts. The Old Testament indicates that God gave some people spiritual gifts before the coming of Christ (Exodus 28:2-3; 35:31-32; 2 Kings 2:9-10), and the New Testament records that the disciples served through their gifts from the Holy Spirit during the earthly ministry of Jesus (Matthew 10:1; Mark 3:13-15). Not until the outpouring of the Spirit at Pentecost did the gifts of the Spirit flourish. After being filled with the Holy Spirit, the Christians' sensitivity and openness to spiritual gifts increased significantly. Among the gifts that flourished were: healings, prophecies, discernment, wisdom, faith, and the workings of miracles. The Book of Acts leaves no doubt about the gifts of the Spirit abounding among the first Christians after they were filled with the Spirit.

—Be—

The Spirit who inspired the Bible is the same Spirit who empowers us in our witnessing about Jesus. The Bible is the standard for faith and practice. Pentecostal Christians do not worship the Bible, but through the Spirit, the Bible has new life and meaning for them. The Holy Spirit confirms the authority of the Bible to their hearts and gives to them spiritual grasp of the words and deeds of Scripture. Pentecostals are not only to be people of the Spirit, but also people of the Book. Spirit baptism increases our desire to study God's Word and to live by it.

Baptism in the Spirit deepens our reverence for the Father, the Son, and the Holy Spirit. Living in this fullness of the Spirit intensifies our hearts cry, "Abba, Father" (Romans 8:15; Galatians 4:6) and increases our awareness of the realty of Jesus and His lordship over us (Acts 2:36; 7:55). This experience gives us great assurance that the Holy Spirit has poured God's love and power into our hearts (Romans 5:5; Acts 1:8). Therefore, being filled with the Spirit enhances our prayer life and our praise and worship of the triune God.

Consider:

- What helps you to be open and sensitive to the manifestation of spiritual gifts?

- How does your religious background influence your view of baptism in the Spirit and gifts of the Spirit?

- As you have worked through this series of lessons, have you seen any change in your life or belief? If so, in what way?

—Do—

The Bible teaches believers to examine carefully that which is claimed to be of the Spirit (1 Thessalonians 5:19-21). The gifts of the Spirit are important, and the Spirit gives us a sensitivity to spiritual things, but Christians are not to believe every spiritual manifestation is from the Holy Spirit. Believers are to "test the spirits, whether they are of God" (1 John 4:1).

That is done by answering the following questions:

- Does the manifestation exalt Christ?
- Does the manifestation edify the church?
- Does the person who speaks or acts do it in love?
- Is Jesus the Lord of the person's life through whom a manifestation operates?
- Is the person willing for mature Christians to evaluate what has been said or done?

- If it is a predictive word, then is it fulfilled?

  (Arrington, *Encountering the Holy Spirit,* pp. 259-60).

Consider the church today:

- What might hinder some Christians from being open to the gifts of the Spirit?

- How might we encourage others to use their gifts?

- How might we show that we value all gifts of the Spirit?

Offer a Prayer

Heavenly Father, thank You for Your gifts that You give us through Your Holy Spirit. Help me to be sensitive to the Spirit and open to using the Spiritual gifts that You give me. I want to glorify You always. In Jesus' name I pray. Amen.

Day 3

Greater Consecration to God

Searching the Scripture

Read Acts 9:31

> Then the churches throughout all Judea, Galilee, and Samaria had peace and were edified. And walking in the fear of the Lord and in the comfort of the Holy Spirit, they were multiplied.

Answer the Following Questions:

1. What does it mean to be *consecrated to God* (devoted, dedicated to God)? (See: Acts 9:31; 6:4; Romans 12:1; 1 Chronicles 29:5; 2 Timothy 2:21; Psalm 51:17; Philippians 2:8 [Jesus]; John 13:34-35).

    Set apart

2. Consecration to God involves humility. Explain why having a particular spiritual experience (like *being baptized in the Holy Spirit*) or coming from a particular Christian tradition (like *Pentecostalism*) or having a particular spiritual gift (like *teaching, interpretation of tongues,* or *prophecy*) does not make one Christian better than another. (See: Romans 12:3; Philippians 2:1-3; Galatians 5:25-26; 6:4; 1 Corinthians 12:4-6; 13:1-13.)

3. How do the blessings of the Holy Spirit help us live consecrated lives of love—giving ourselves and our lives to God daily, and loving our neighbors?

Yielding to the Spirit

—*Know*—

A blessing for all of life. The filling with the Spirit impacts the whole life of the believer. Therefore, Spirit baptism complements both the saving and sanctifying work of the Holy Spirit. From Pentecost on, the Spirit made a remarkable difference in the life of the early disciples. The Pentecostal experience has resulted in a deeper consecration to God and greater devotion to His Word.

For the early Christians, that experience enhanced the whole process of their being Christians. Because of what they received on the Day of Pentecost, they were keenly aware of the Spirit's guidance (Acts 4:8-12; 6:5; 9:31; 10:19). All believers, past and present, who have received the Pentecostal blessing have come under the profound influence of the Holy Spirit.

—*Be*—

After the outpouring of the Spirit at Pentecost, there emerged a community of faith whose life was lived according to the Spirit of holiness. This new community steadfastly devoted themselves to the apostles' teachings about Christ, and to deep fellowship, to the breaking of bread in the Lord's Supper, and to prayer (Acts 2:42). Jesus had said, "you will be My disciples" (John 15:8). That is precisely what early believers became and God desires all Christians to be. Spirit-filled people should not be "on and off" Christians. People who are devoted to following Jesus daily, through the Holy Spirit's guidance and power, will grow and over time increase in their ability to follow God's ways in all of life.

Consider:

- What is an important truth that you have learned in this study about the Holy Spirit that will help you live a more consecrated life?

- What helps you to hear the voice of the Holy Spirit as you read and study the Bible, and as you go about your daily activities?

—Do—

Living devoted to God. The Holy Spirit is "the Spirit of holiness" (Romans 1:4). Believers who maintain Spirit-filled lives are those who live according to the Spirit (Galatians 5:22-23). They take no pleasure in sin and ungodly pursuits, and they strive to avoid selfishness. In all matters, they desire to love God and others.

The Spirit of peace. We have emphasized spiritual power for witnessing, doing mighty works, and withstanding persecution from a hostile world. But let us remember that the Holy Spirit is also the Spirit of peace (Galatians 5:22), and is very much present in the church when there may be troubles and small storms among believers. The Spirit sees all that goes on in the church, and through Jesus Christ, wants to bring wisdom and healing to the church in all circumstances.

The Spirit who guides. It is easy for Christians to become distracted by the many demanding and interesting things of this world. This can result in our being diverted from living out our mission of a holy (consecrated, devoted) life, and telling the story of the gospel (the good news about the love of Jesus Christ). Through the Holy Spirit, we learn in all areas of life to focus on the things of God and His love.

Consider:

- What are some things we can do to help us live our purpose?

Offer a Prayer

Heavenly Father, thank You that through Jesus Christ and the power of the Holy Spirit, You forgive and heal us from the sin, darkness, and chaos in our lives. Please help me to live a life consecrated to You. Fill me daily with the Spirit's blessings, so that I may walk every moment in humility and love with Jesus my Lord. Amen.

Day 4

Greater Joy

Searching the Scripture

Read Acts 13:52

> And the disciples were filled with joy and with the Holy Spirit.

Answer the Following Questions:

1. To learn more about what *joy* through Jesus Christ and the blessings of the Holy Spirit is, read a few Scripture passages (or all, if you like) in each of the following categories.

Joy of the Lord	
True life with the Father and Jesus Christ	Luke 2:10; 6:23; John 15:9-11; Acts 2:25-28; Romans 5:10-11; Hebrews 12:2; Jude 1:24-25
The presence and blessings of the Holy Spirit	Psalm 51:10-13; Acts 8:4-8; 13:48-49, 52; Romans 5:1-5; 14:16-17; Galatians 5:22-23; Colossians 1:9-11; 1 Thessalonians 1:6
God's Word	Matthew 13:20; Luke 8:13; John 1:14
Fellowship in the body of Christ (the church)	Acts 2:43-47 and 2 Corinthians 8:1-5 (generosity and hospitality); Philemon 1:20 (encouragement); 1 Thessalonians 2:18-20 (together in the presence of Jesus)
Prayer, worship, and thanksgiving	Psalm 33:3; 95:2; 98:1-9; Isaiah 61:10; Acts 1:12-14; 16:25
Living focused on the things of God	Psalm 32:11; 89:15; Matthew 25:23; John 15:9-11
Hope and perseverance in difficulties	Matthew 5:12; Romans 5:1-5; James 1:2-4; 1 Peter 1:6-9; 4:13-14; Psalm 94:19

2. Which of the Scripture passages above really speaks to your heart today? Describe why this passage is especially meaningful to you.

3. Why do you think that Paul listed "*joy*" as a vital fruit of the Spirit (Galatians 5:22)?

4. Can you explain why joy brought by the Holy Spirit runs deeper than pain or pleasure, and is not limited by external circumstances?

5. Pentecostals often express their joy as they worship by praising, singing, shouting, clapping, and dancing in the Spirit. Why do you think they do this?

Yielding to the Spirit

—Know—

Joy from the Holy Spirit. The gift of the Spirit brought great joy to the hearts of Jesus' disciples. On the Day of Pentecost, there was rejoicing in the Lord as they spoke about "the wonderful works of God" (Acts 2:11). Some accused them of being "full of new wine" (v. 13), but the truth was they were full of the Spirit and were experiencing joy that flooded their whole being. So it is understandable why "they ate their food with gladness" (Acts 2:46). Furthermore, at Antioch "the disciples were filled with joy and with the Holy Spirit" (13:52).

Joy in adversity. Great joy comes with immersion in the Spirit. It is a joy that is deep and abiding. It remains through adverse circumstances. For example, the apostles were jailed, beaten, and forbidden by the Jewish council to speak in the name of Jesus. But when they were released, "they departed from the presence of the council, rejoicing that they were counted worthy to suffer shame for His name" (5:41). This kind of joy did not fade in the face of adversity and persecution. Out of the baptism in the Spirit comes the fullness of joy—"joy inexpressible and full of glory" (1 Peter 1:8).

Faith and joy. Joy is a vital result of faith and opens hearts to the praise, thanksgiving, and worship of God. Such joy flows out of a profound sense of the Spirit's presence. Even before Pentecost, the disciples experienced joy (Luke 24:41). But after Pentecost, they came to know the fullness of joy. Paul prayed for believers to be filled with "all joy . . . by the power of the Holy Spirit" (Roman 15:13). The immediate and abiding effect of immersion in the Spirit is deeper joy.

—Be—

On the Day of Pentecost, the 120 disciples experienced great joy and vigor in the Spirit. They began to pour forth praise and thanksgiving to God for His mighty saving acts in Christ. Full of the joy of the Spirit, they became a powerful prophetic, charismatic community of worshipers. This community of faith became known for its single-hearted devotion, and was highly favored by many people.

Spiritual joy is not always experienced as a happy feeling, but sometimes as: knowing, trusting, placing one's hope, or persevering (not giving up).

Consider:

- In your own life what brings you lasting joy?

- Do you have some ideas for how you might nurture your spiritual joy when times are not easy—to help you persevere during hard times?

- Also, what might you do in the midst of a crisis or in ongoing difficult circumstances to help you abide in real spiritual joy? Might part of this be seeking help from others and spending time with people in your church fellowship?

—*Do*—

The baptism of the Holy Spirit prompts believers to be generous in many ways. Their expressions to others of the joy of the Lord takes many forms, such as: worship, verbal testimony, the arts, encouragement, hospitality, compassion, and caring.

For the early Christians, the meals in their homes were joyful occasions and expressed their love for one another (Acts 2:43-47). Also, Jesus Christ's compassion toward the needy inspired them to minister to the critical needs of others (Acts 2:44-45; 3:1-10; 4:34-35; 9:36). They actually sold their goods when needs arose. These early followers of Jesus are marvelous examples for Spirit-filled Christians today. Our joy in serving the Lord should be marked by our generosity to the poor, homeless, and social outcasts.

Consider:

- How do you want to express joy in your church fellowship, among your family and friends, and in the world?

Offer a Prayer

Holy Spirit, You give me love, joy, and peace. Help me to abide in the joy of my Lord Jesus in both happy and difficult times. Teach me how to show Your joy and to encourage others in theirs. Amen.

Day 5

Greater Comfort

Searching the Scripture

Jesus speaking to His disciples:

Read John 14:16, 26 (KJV)

> And I will pray the Father, and he shall give you another Comforter, that he may abide with you forever.
>
> But the Comforter, which is the Holy Ghost, whom the Father will send in my name, he shall teach you all things, and bring all things to your remembrance, whatsoever I have said unto you.

Read John 15:26 (KJV)

> But when the Comforter is come, whom I will send unto you from the Father, even the Spirit of truth, which proceedeth from the Father, he shall testify of me.

Answer the Following Questions:

1. In John 13:33-36 and 14:1-31, during the Passover meal before Jesus was crucified on the cross, He prepares His disciples for what is ahead. Why do you think that Jesus tells them that He will pray that God will give them "another Comforter"?

2. The Greek word for "*Comforter*" is *Parakletos*, which can mean *comforter, counselor, advocate* or *helper*. In the early church following the Day of Pentecost, in what circumstances might the Holy Spirit have provided comfort? Examples: *Peter and John* (Acts 4:3-22; 5:17-42); *Stephen* (6:8–7:60); *James and Peter* (12:1-5); *many Christians* (8:3; 9:2); *Paul, who became a Christian after Jesus' death and resurrection, and Paul's companions* (chapters 13-28).

3. Considering: (1) how the Holy Spirit helped the early Christians (book of Acts), (2) the fruit of the Spirit that all Christians are given (Galatians 5:22-23), and (3) the Holy Spirit's help during our prayers (Romans 8:26-27), why do you think it is appropriate to speak of the Holy Spirit as "*the Comforter*"?

Yielding to the Spirit

—Know—

The Holy Spirit as *the Comforter*. Jesus earthly ministry came to a close when He ascended into heaven. Before He departed, the Savior promised His disciples that He would send them the Holy Spirit as their Comforter (*parakletos*). The Greek word for *Comforter* occurs several times in the gospel of John (in chapters 14-16) and can mean *comforter*, *counselor*, *advocate* or *helper*. As Jesus did while He was on earth, the Holy Spirit now brings peace and consolation to those who follow Jesus. So it is appropriate to speak of the Holy Spirit as "*the Comforter*," since the Spirit is the One who acts on behalf of Jesus.

Fellowship with the Holy Spirit. The Spirit has been called to dwell in God's people and to accompany them through all of life (Romans 8:9). His role is to bring Jesus to believers and to give them emotional support and spiritual help and power.

The disciples, when they went to Jerusalem to observe the festival of Pentecost, had already dedicated their lives to Jesus Christ, and they had the Holy Spirit (*the Comforter*) dwelling within them. Prior to Pentecost, Jesus had said to His disciples: "The Spirit of truth...you know Him, for He dwells with you and will be in you" (John 14:17). They had fellowship with the Holy Spirit.

The Spirit's special anointing of comfort and courage. On the Day of Pentecost as the disciples of Jesus were praying, they received a fresh experience of the Spirit, a special anointing. "They were all filled with the Holy Spirit" (Acts 2:4). Through this anointing, they received a greater sense of who they were, and greater assurance of what God wanted them to do. The receiving of the fullness of the Spirit on the Day of Pentecost gave these early followers of Jesus greater comfort and confidence.

Jesus had challenged His disciples to take the gospel to the ends of the earth (Acts 1:8). Throughout the book of Acts, Luke tells the story of the forward spread of the gospel from Jerusalem to the city of Rome. The first Spirit-filled believers encountered great opposition as they told others the Good News about the resurrection of Jesus and the life He offers. As those believers testified about the saving grace of Jesus, their enemies sought to discourage them by persecuting them. But the Holy Spirit gave them comfort and courage to live out their faith under the lordship of Jesus their Savior (Acts 4:5-22; 5:17-42; 7:54–8:3; 9:1-9). Great comfort flowed from the fullness of the Spirit. As these early believers were being persecuted and humiliated, the Spirit's comfort and encouragement kept their trust in the Lord alive.

The Spirit's comfort in our lives. Today the Comforter carries on the work of Jesus in a world that often contradicts and is hostile toward the love, grace, and peace of God. In so doing, the Spirit bears witness concerning the life and teachings of Jesus. The Spirit's witness is always truthful for He is *"the Spirit of truth"* (John 14:17; 15:26). He never misleads anyone. In Jesus' days on the earth, He walked alongside His followers as their *Comforter* and *Counselor*. Having taken Jesus' place here, the Holy Spirit comforts believers by assuring them they are children of God. The Spirit abides with them daily guiding and blessing them

There is an old hymn that has a great message of assurance. It says, *"He abides, He abides. Hallelujah, He abides with me!"* (Buffum and Shanks, 1922). Indeed, the Holy Spirit does abide with us and gives us the same comfort and assurance that Jesus did.

—Be—

The Holy Spirit's presence in our troubles. A wide range of needs exist in the church and in the lives of individual Christians. Each of us has our own struggles. We may struggle with various personal day-to-day challenges, such as: heartache when family members or others do not our life of faith; pain and suffering from illness or other problems; or conflicts within the culture in which we live. There are many throughout the world who are in real danger due to their beliefs about Jesus. Such dangers include various types of discrimination, physical and mental abuse, loss of job, criminal charges, or even death. Regardless of our circumstances, like the followers of Jesus in the early church who faced great persecution and troubles, we have a Comforter who is with us at all times.

Awareness of the presence of the Holy Spirit. As we read the book of Acts, we can learn from the lives of the early Christians, who had deep awareness of the presence of the Holy Spirit. This awareness grew out of their submitting to the blessings and fullness of the Holy Spirit. It was through their anointing on the Day of Pentecost that they received the comforting fellowship, guidance, and powerful presence of the Holy Spirit. They had an awareness of God's presence and blessings in their lives, in spite of their adversities.

Today followers of Jesus, like His early followers on the Day of Pentecost, we can receive the fullness of the Spirit and can experience daily the comforting fellowship of the Holy Spirit. For "the Spirit Himself bears witness with our spirit that we are children of God" (Romans 8:16). As we face adversities and temptations, we, too, must be aware that we have the Comforter in our hearts. Regardless of our circumstances, the Holy Spirit gives us the assurance that we are God's children.

Consider:

- If there have been times in your life in which the Holy Spirit has comforted you? Maybe you didn't recognize His presence at that time, but now you see that He was there helping you.

- Did you experience the Spirit as your *comforter, counselor, advocate* or *helper*?

- When praying, have you ever been at a loss for words to express what was in your heart—then you experienced the comforting hand of the Holy Spirit, praying through you on your behalf? How did that feel?

—Do—

Inviting the Comforter to work in our lives and the life of the church. How do we go about living a life in the fullness of the *comfort* of the Holy Spirit? We can do this by inviting the Holy Spirit into all areas of our personal life and the life of the church. By making space in our lives to be still and to pray and listen to God, we open up opportunities for the Holy Spirit to minister to us.

Inviting the Holy Spirit to comfort us during our prayers.-In our prayers, when we cry out to the Father, the Holy Spirit intercedes on our behalf. (Romans 8:26). When we are weak and carrying heavy burdens and facing painful and unpredictable circumstances, we may not know how to pray, but the Holy Spirit knows how. During these times in which there are "groanings," which are too deep to be expressed in human words, the Holy Spirit may pray through us using tongues. What then must we do? Be open to Holy Spirit and His guidance and prayers.

The Holy Spirit's comfort and our comfort of others. The Holy Spirit helps us walk in clarity and peace, rather than relying our own faulty human reasoning. It is good for us to remember that the

Comforter is also our mentor and that He not only comforts us, but enables us to comfort others out of the great overflow of comfort that the Spirit gives to us. (Wayne Brewer, unpublished notes, 2017).

Consider:

- How have you seen the Holy Spirit minister comfort in the life of your church fellowship?

- Are there ways that the Holy Spirit has used you to bring comfort?

- Are there ways you would like the Holy Spirit to use you?

Offer a Prayer

Jesus, You bring us comfort through the Holy Spirit. Help us to lean on the Spirit for comfort, counsel, and help in all circumstances of our lives and the life of the church. Amen.

Group Discussion

Key Scripture—Acts 2:17-18

> And it shall come to pass in the last days, says God, "That I will pour out of My Spirit on all flesh; your sons and your daughters shall prophesy, Your young men shall see visions, your old men shall dream dreams. And on My menservants and on My maidservants I will pour out My Spirit in those days; and they shall prophesy" (Acts 2:17-18).

Opening—This is a time of fellowship and sharing about one another's lives.

Prayer

Testimony—Have two or three group members give a testimony of how God is at work in their lives, whether it is through their daily encounters in this study, or some other way.

Discussion Questions:

1. What did the outpouring of the Holy Spirit enable the early disciples to do? List at least three and explain their significance for today.

2. Explain the significance of the anointing of the Spirit
    making believers more sensitive and open to gifts of
    the Spirit and their use.

3. What does the following statement mean: *The filling
    with the Spirit impacts the whole life of the believer*?

4. Explain the significance of the phrase "*the Spirit of holiness*" (1:4 Romans).

5. We experience great joy when immersed in the Spirit. Explain why this kind of joy does not fade away when one faces adversity or persecution.

6. Give evidence from the Scriptures that the early Christians were generous people.

7. How should we understand the prayer ministry of the Holy Spirit in light of Romans 8:28?

8. In this week's study about *the Results of Being Baptized in the Holy Spirit*, what has impacted you the most?

Closing Prayer

THE

HOLY SPIRIT

IN THE LIFE OF THE

CHURCH

Week 4

Day 1
The Spirit and
the Laying on of Hands

DECLARATION OF FAITH

"We Believe . . .

In the baptism with the Holy Ghost subsequent to a clean heart."

"We Believe . . .

In speaking with other tongues as the Spirit gives utterance and that it is the initial evidence of the baptism of the Holy Ghost."

Words to Hide in Your Heart

"The Spirit of the Lord is upon Me, because He has anointed Me to preach the gospel to the poor; He has sent Me to heal the brokenhearted, to proclaim liberty to the captives and recovery of sight to the blind, to set at liberty those who are oppressed; to proclaim the acceptable year of the Lord" (Luke 4:18-19).

Touching Base

We have focused on the baptism in the Spirit—particularly the initial evidence—what prepares one to receive this baptism, and the results of it. Now we turn to other matters that are related to the baptism in the Spirit: (1) the laying on of hands, (2) the role of speaking in tongues in worship services, (3) the last days, and (4) a brief history of the Pentecostal movement.

Searching the Scripture

Read Acts 8:14-17

Now when the apostles who were at Jerusalem heard that Samaria had received the word of God, they sent Peter and John to them, who, when they had come down, prayed for them that they might receive the Holy Spirit. For as yet He had fallen upon none of them. They had only been baptized in the name of the Lord Jesus. Then they laid hands on them, and they received the Holy Spirit.

Answer the Following Questions:

1. Ananias, an ordinary Christian, laid his hands on Saul (Paul), and Paul was filled with the Spirit. What does this tell about the status and position of those who practice the laying on of hands when they pray for others? (See Acts 9:10-19.)

2. When Christians pray for a person through the laying on of hands and that person receives the fullness of the Holy Spirit, where does this blessing come from?

3. Since a person's praying for another has no special power to transfer the Holy Spirit, what purpose do you think the laying on of hands serves? (See "*Know*" section.)

4. Why may the laying on of hands make it easier for some believers to be filled with the Spirit?

5. Spirit-filled worship often includes several believers gathering around a person and the laying on of hands with prayer. Why is this an important element of corporate worship?

Yielding to the Spirit

—Know—

Let us look more closely at the matter of *laying on of hands*. Within the Christian community, *laying on of hands* is a form of active prayer that is done to invite God's blessings through the healing presence of Jesus and the empowering presence of the Holy Spirit. This type of prayer communicates compassion, consecration, and honor. It is most often done in a worship setting, in which followers of Jesus pray for a person and that person's needs, or when individuals are being confirmed, ordained, or commissioned for ministry.

Laying on of hands and the fullness of the Holy Spirit. Specifically, what is the relation of this action to receiving the fullness of the Spirit? We are not told of anyone who prayed for the disciples in Jerusalem or Caesarea using the laying on of hands. (Acts 2;10). Peter was present in Caesarea and could have laid hands on the ones who were filled with the Spirit. However, this act of prayer was not needed, since God filled them with the Spirit immediately, and gave to them tongues (*glossolalia*), which showed that they had been filled with the Spirit.

The Book of Acts does indicate three occasions in which people received the laying on of hands—those people being the Samaritans, the apostle Paul, and the twelve followers of Jesus in Ephesus. When Peter and John arrived in Samaria, they prayed for the believers and "then they laid hands on them, and they received the Holy Spirit" (Acts 8:16-17). After Paul prayed for three days, Ananias laid hands on him; and he was filled with Holy Spirit (9:17). In regard to the twelve at Ephesus, as Paul laid hands on them, "the Holy Spirit came upon them, and they spoke with tongues and prophesied" (19:6).

Evidently, there is no essential connection between the laying on of hands and receiving the Holy Spirit. But why is there a difference—some having human mediation and others not? The disciples in Jerusalem and the believers in Caesarea, who had been dedicating themselves to prayer and obedience to God, were filled with the Spirit immediately. On the other hand, the Samaritans, Ephesian twelve, and Paul most likely needed the support of others. For them, the laying on of hands would have provided the prayerful encouragement and care that they needed.

Guidance for praying using laying on of hands. A few observations are in order here: (1) Prayer and obedience are more foundational than the laying on of hands for reception of the Holy Spirit. (2) The laying on of hands symbolizes that the person is submissive to receiving a fresh work of God. (3) Human hands cannot impart the supernatural gift. Regardless of how devout a person may be, this act of placing hands on someone lacks any special power to transfer the Holy Spirit. The touching may reach the faith of the one who is prepared to be filled with the Spirit. In that case, the human agent is the channel of God's grace.

The laying on of hands is in order if the person is comfortable with it, but not always necessary. It is important that in the laying on of hands, we always take into consideration the emotional and physical needs of the person for whom we are praying. In situations where there is physical pain, trauma, or cultural differences, other types of prayer may be best. When praying for someone, it is always important to communicate, and to love and be respectful of each other.

—Be—

God has promised to pour out His Spirit in "the last days." We are living in extraordinary times and are witnesses to a worldwide outpouring of the Spirit. People's personal obedience to God's love and seeking God's will and blessings are important aspects of this outpouring. Also important are our prayers and care for others. As we pray, the laying on of hands may be part of this, as we ask for God's blessings to be poured into the life of another.

Consider:

- What has been your experience with the laying on of hands?

- Do you feel comfortable telling other people who care and want to pray for you, what type of prayer you feel you need?

- After studying this lesson, would you like in a worship service, for someone to pray for you to receive a special blessing from the Holy Spirit?

—Do—

The disciples before Pentecost were an expectant people. They waited and prayed. After they were filled with the Spirit, Peter assured them that the outpouring of the Spirit was not a once-in-a-lifetime event. The promise of the Spirit is for all who come to faith in Christ.

As we pray for people and ask God to bless them, it is important to remember that God may use or may not use the laying on of hands. God remains free to give the Holy Spirit as He wills. On the human side, our trust in God is vital to receiving the full blessings of the Holy Spirit. Also, when we pray for others, it is important for us to have faith and to listen to God's guidance. But when all is said, God is the Giver of the Spirit, and on some occasions, He uses human mediation (through the laying on of hands) to accomplish His will.

Offer a Prayer

Holy Spirit, thank You for all your blessings. Thank You for the people who pray for me. Help me to know how best to pray for them. Help me to cherish God's Word and to follow Jesus in all things. In the name of Jesus Christ, I pray. Amen.

Day 2

The Role of Speaking in Tongues in Public Worship

Searching the Scripture

Read 1 Corinthians 14:2 and 12:7-11:

Tongues as personal prayer to God:
For he who speaks in a tongue does not speak to men but to God, for no one understands him; however, in the spirit he speaks mysteries.

Tongues and interpretation as gifts of the Spirit for instruction and encouragement in the church community:
But the manifestation of the Spirit is given to each one for the profit of all: for to one is given the word of wisdom through the Spirit, to another the word of knowledge through the same Spirit, to another faith by the same Spirit, to another gifts of healings by the same Spirit, to another the working of miracles, to another prophecy, to another discerning of spirits, to another different kinds of

tongues, to another the interpretation of tongues. But one and the same Spirit works all these things, distributing to each one individually as He wills.

Answer the Following Questions:

1. Read through the Appendix: "*Spiritual Purposes of Speaking in Tongues (Glossolalia): 1 Corinthians chapters 12, 13, and 14*" located in the back of this book. What differences are there between the gift of tongues and speaking in tongues in private prayer and worship?

2. When we pray in tongues in our private devotions, what does that do for us?

3. When we welcome the gift of speaking in tongues followed by interpretation into our worship, what does that do for us and our church fellowship?

Yielding to the Spirit

—Know—

The apostle Paul had a deep concern about the community life of the church and that what is done in corporate worship be clear and understandable. In 1 Corinthians 14, he emphasized that in a worship gathering, speaking in tongues should be followed by interpretation. Without interpretation, the congregation would not understand or be built up spiritually.

Speaking in tongues devotionally. Paul does not go into great detail, but in reading 1 Corinthians 14:4, it does seem that he would endorse the Holy Spirit breaking into corporate worship in a more devotional way that may include prayer and praise in tongues without interpretation. This type of prayer would involve individuals praying in the Spirit to God at the same time, but using different words. This type of prayer is most likely to occur during points in a worship gathering that are set aside specifically for devotional prayer, waiting on God, or praying for others. This prayer time is traditionally called in Pentecostal churches "*altar call*" or "*altar service.*" At that point, the worship is less structured and lends itself more to devotional worship.

Even though individuals are personally devotional in a group setting, their prayers together can have a unifying effect on the gathered body of Christ. To lead Pentecostal worship (which includes speaking in tongues, interpretation of those tongues, and devotional prayers and tongues) requires a great deal of wisdom and guidance. As in all matters of worship, we want to remain focused on God's love through Jesus, and do what is spiritually beneficial for each other.

Differences in the purpose of tongues. The focus here is on the different uses of tongues. There may be a lack of understanding of the difference of speaking in tongues as initial evidence, as a prayer and praise language, and as one of the spiritual gifts. What we want to do is to note the differences so that we can understand and apply this teaching to our worship and lives.

To begin, a couple of terms are important. (1) *Speaking in tongues (glossolalia)* refers to unknown languages or "the tongues of men and of angels" inspired by the Holy Spirit (1 Corinthians 13:1). (2) The term *zenolalia* refers to "tongues of men," that is, known human languages that are coupled with the power of the Holy Spirit. Such languages are unknown to the speaker, but may be known by someone present. The only biblical record we have of this special form of speaking in tongues is Acts 2:5-12. The Jews from every nation understood the languages spoken by the Galilean disciples on Pentecost. There are credible reports that the Holy Spirit has worked in this manner over the years.

Tongues linked with power of Spirit, whether they be *glossolalia* or *zenolalia,* may function as the initial evidence. Since initial evidence doctrine has already been discussed in this study, at this point we turn to tongues as prayer and praise, and as one of the gifts of the Spirit.

Tongues as prayer and praise language:

Praying in tongues creates intimate communion with God:

"For he who speaks in tongues does not speak to men but to God, for no one understands him; however, in the spirit he speaks mysteries. . . . He who speaks in tongues edifies himself" (1 Corinthians 14:2, 4).

- Praying in tongues is biblical.

- We speak to God.

- We utter mysteries by the Spirit.

- The individual builds himself/herself up spiritually.

> Likewise the Spirit also helps in our weaknesses. For we do not know what we should pray for as we ought, but the Spirit Himself makes intercession for us with groanings which cannot be uttered. Now He who searches the hearts knows what the mind of the Spirit is, because He makes intercession for the saints according to the will of God (Romans 8:26-27).

- The word "*groaning*" most likely refers to the Spirit praying through believers in tongues.

- The Spirit helps us because we do not always know how we should pray.

- The Spirit always prays correctly because He knows the perfect will of God.

- By prayer in tongues, the believer makes the decision to cooperate with the Holy Spirit.

- All Spirit-filled believers may have a prayer language in tongues.

Tongues as one of the gifts of the Spirit:

> But the manifestation of the Spirit is given to each one for the profit of all: for to one is given the word of wisdom

through the Spirit . . . to another different kinds of tongues, to another the interpretation of tongues. But one and the same Spirit works all these things, distributing to each one individually as He wills (1 Corinthians 12:7-11).

- The Holy Spirit distributes spiritual gifts as He wills to maintain a balance of ministry in the church.

- The companion gift for the gift of tongues is interpretation.

- A person who has the gift of tongues builds up the church provided his/her message in tongues is interpreted.

- All Spirit-filled believers do not have the gift of tongues for the building up of the church. The Holy Spirit decides who receives what gift or gifts.

—Be—

Someone has called Romans chapter 8 "the Pentecost" of the great letter. Throughout this chapter, Paul emphasizes the ministry of the Holy Spirit in the life of believers. Particularly from verse 26 onward, the focus is on the importance of Christian discipleship in which there is the constant guidance of the Holy Spirit through prayer. Often our primary weakness is that we do not know how to pray. Every child of God needs to be mentored by the Holy Spirit so that we can grow and learn to have the mind of the Spirit, that is, learn to be in agreement with the Holy Spirit in our prayers, our thinking, and our lives.

Consider:

- What have been your experiences with speaking in tongues?

- How do you feel about those experiences?

—*Do*—

The apostle Paul says that the Spirit makes intercession for us "according to the will of God" (Romans 8:27). "*The will of God*" refers to the will of the Father. The Father's will is that we be spiritually formed to the likeness of God's Son (v. 29). What we need to do is to pray to know what the Holy Spirit is desiring to do (the Spirit's mind), for the Spirit knows the will of the Father. As we follow the leading of the Holy Spirit, we will be conformed to the likeness of God's Son, Jesus Christ.

Consider:

- How do you think your church fellowship can invite the Holy Spirit into its times of worship and prayer, and discern what the Spirit desires to do?

- How might focusing on love through Jesus Christ help?

- How might the gift of tongues and devotional tongues be part of your church's worship?

Offer a Prayer

Jesus, You work in miraculous ways in the church through the Holy Spirit. Holy Spirit, I pray for my church fellowship now, that we will be open to You and Your voice. Speak to us and through us, so that we may glorify God in all we say and do. Amen.

Day 3
The Spirit and the End Time

Searching the Scripture

Read Acts 2:17-19 (See also Joel 2:28-32):

> And it shall come to pass in the last days, says God, that I will pour out of My Spirit on all flesh; your sons and your daughters shall prophesy, your young men shall see visions, your old men shall dream dreams. And on My menservants and on My maidservants I will pour out My Spirit in those days; and they shall prophesy. I will show wonders in heaven above and signs in the earth beneath.

Answer the Following Questions:

1. "The last days" began with the ministry of Jesus and the outpouring of the Spirit on the Day of Pentecost. What are the signs that the end of time may be near?

2. What do you think "groanings too deep for words" refers to (Romans 8:26 MEV).

3. Why do you think we need the Holy Spirit during the times in which we live?

Yielding to the Spirit

—*Know*—

The Last Days / End Time. Acts 2:17 states that "in the last days," God "will pour out" His Spirit on all people. *The Last Days* is the era that began on Pentecost, which is to conclude in what we commonly call *the End Time* or *End Times.* The End Time is a time period in which world events will reach a final climax—Christ will come to earth again, and will reign on the earth for a thousand years. Many Christians believe that we are now living in the final days of the End Time.

The Day of Pentecost and the Last Days. The coming of the Holy Spirit on the Day of Pentecost and other events of the Last Days had been predicted by the prophet Joel (2:17-19). This immersion/baptism in the Spirit of which Joel had prophesied was and continues to be an empowering experience. The audible, visible sign of speaking in tongues accompanied this experience. This sign was not only evidence of one's being filled with the Spirit, but it also served to introduce a new era of the Spirit. Some call speaking in tongues "a prayer language," which underscores its personal and devotional character for this age in which we live (1 Corinthians 14:4-5; 16-17).

As the modern-day Pentecostal Movement has developed, one of the distinctive marks has been a fervent expectation that Christ could return at any time to wrap up world history. Therefore, there has been a strong conviction that the second coming of Christ has been at hand, and because of that, there has been urgency to spread the gospel. Now we are in the twenty-first century and Christ has not returned. But even so, there seem to be many signs that indicate that the coming of Christ is very near. We must be in the last chapter of time, but we do not know how long that chapter will be. It looks like the end may come soon.

Biblical spirituality holds in tension the presence of God's kingdom in this world, and the future hope of the coming of the kingdom's fullness. *The doctrine of last things* is very important to us Pentecostals and helps us to have a fervent expectation of the fullness of the Kingdom to come.

—Be—

Like the early Pentecostals, we need to live in expectancy for the coming of Jesus Christ. As we prepare our own hearts for His second coming, we also need to be committed to reaching as many souls as possible with Jesus' good news—so that they, too, can be ready.

Consider:

- How do you feel about living in the End Time, and the possibility that Jesus could return in your lifetime?

- Do you think that our experiences of baptism in the Holy Spirit and speaking in other tongues might give us a foretaste of the kingdom to come?

- Do you long for that day?

—Do—

Since the time must be short, it is imperative that we embrace a lifestyle that is pleasing to our Savior, and worship in a manner that does not quench the Holy Spirit. A sense of the real presence of God in our worship, anointed leadership, planned church services that are open to divine interruptions, and preaching with solid biblical content will not offend the Holy Spirit, but will please Him. These actions will also spiritually prepare God's people for the coming of Christ.

Offer a Prayer

Holy Spirit, You came on the Day of Pentecost to fill and empower us in these Last Days. Fill me and help me to fix my eyes on God's kingdom, and to reflect His kingdom "on earth as it is in heaven." Help me to live expectant of my Lord Jesus' return. Amen.

Day 4

The Relationship Between Gifts of the Spirit and Fruit of the Spirit

Searching the Scripture

Gifts of the Spirit:

Read 1 Corinthians 12:8-10

For to one is given the word of wisdom through the Spirit, to another the word of knowledge through the same Spirit, to another faith by the same Spirit, to another gifts of healings by the same Spirit, to another the working of miracles, to another prophecy, to another discerning of spirits, to another different kinds of tongues, to another the interpretation of tongues.

Fruit of the Spirit:

Read Galatians 5:22-23

But the fruit of the Spirit is love, joy, peace, longsuffering, kindness, goodness, faithfulness, gentleness, self-control. Against such there is no law.

Answer the Following Questions:

1. What are *gifts of the Spirit* (spiritual gifts) and *fruit of the Spirit* (spiritual fruit)?

2. Who receives these blessings? *Gifts* (1 Corinthians 12:7-11; *Fruit* (Galatians 5: 22-23)

3. Read these four lists of the *gifts of the Spirit* in the New Testament: Romans 12:6-8; 1 Corinthians 12:8-10; Ephesians 4:11; and 1 Peter 4:11. What impacts you most about these lists?

4. The Holy Spirit transforms believers and works His *fruit* into them by infusion. Identify a number of the *fruit of the Spirit*, and explain your thoughts about how the Holy's Spirit's process of infusion causes the fruit of the Spirit to permeate all of life.

5. Are spiritual gifts only granted to those who are spiritually mature? Discuss your answer in light of 1 Corinthians chapters 12-14.

6. Why should we understand that the gifts are not limited to church leaders (1 Corinthians 12:7-11)?

Yielding to the Spirit

—Know—

The Holy Spirit blesses and helps followers of Jesus in many ways. The Spirit gives us both *spiritual gifts* and *spiritual fruit*, as well as other blessings, such as *comfort*, *guidance*, and *help* (which have been mentioned earlier in this study).

Definitions. *Fruit of the Spirit* are what God endeavors to do *in* us, namely to conform us to the likeness of Jesus Christ (Galatians 5:22-23). *Love* is the crowning fruit of the Spirit. ***Gifts of the Spirit*** are what God endeavors to do *through* us. A few examples of gifts the Spirit are *healings*, *prophecy*, *a word of wisdom*, *speaking in tongues*, and *interpretation* (1 Corinthians 12:12-28; Arrington, 2003, pp. 250-254).

Gifts of the Holy Spirit. Gifts of the Spirit are mentioned in several passages in both the Old and New Testaments of the Bible. Passages in the New Testament include: Romans 12:6-8; 1 Corinthians 12:8-10; Ephesians 4:11; and 1 Peter 4:11. (For discussion about spiritual gifts in the Old Testament, see *Week 1–Day 5* of this study.)

Among Pentecostals, the list of nine gifts in 1 Corinthians 12:8-10 often receive the most attention and are considered to be the primary list recorded in the New Testament. These gifts are: *the word of wisdom, the word of knowledge, faith, gifts of healings, the working of miracles, prophecy, discerning of spirits, different kinds of tongues,* and *the interpretation of tongues.* First Corinthians 12:28 repeats a number of gifts previously listed in verses 8-10, but this second list adds the gifts of *apostles, teachers, helps,* and *administrations.*

There are three more lists in the New Testament, but they are much briefer. Romans 12:6-8 mentions *prophecy, ministry* (serving others), *teaching, exhortation* (encouragement), *giving* (generosity), *leading* (spiritual guidance and discipleship), and *showing mercy* (compassion ministry and caring for others). The list in Ephesians 4:11 consists of: *apostles, prophets, evangelists,* and *pastor-teachers.* Then the final list in the New Testament, recorded in 1 Peter 4:11, includes only two gifts: *speaking the oracles of God* (the Word of God) and *ministering* (serving).

Through these lists of spiritual gifts, Paul and Peter indicate various types of ministries in the church, but their lists differ from each other. Nowhere in the New Testament is there an effort to list all the gifts of Spirit. Nor do the various lists, if combined, describe the totality of the gifts that are available to God's people. The Holy Spirit does not limit spiritual gifts to the ones listed by Paul and Peter. The Holy Spirit grants many other gifts, such as *intercessory prayer, ministry to children, music, hospitality, various types of creative abilities and skills,* and others. The gifts in any particular list probably spring from the nature of the audience or group to whom Paul or Peter was writing.

Fruit of the Holy Spirit. Like *the gifts of the Spirit, the fruit of the Spirit* are central to the personal lives of individuals and to the ministry of the church. The fruit and the gifts flow from the same Spirit. There is no biblical ground for elevating one over the other. This means that the fruit of the Spirit—*love, joy, peace, longsuffering* (patience, perseverance), *kindness, goodness, faithfulness, gentleness,* and *self-control* (self-discipline) (Galatians 5:22-23)—are as important as the gifts of the Spirit. In fact, we use the spiritual *gifts* we have been given to help us express God's spiritual *fruit.*

God's will and gifts of the Spirit. The Holy Spirit bestows His gifts on individual believers according to His will (1 Corinthians 12:11). All gifts are attached to the

Holy Spirit, and are to operate under His guidance. Gifts of the Spirit are to be used at the direction and the anointing of the Spirit.

Even though spiritual gifts are given to us, we should never lose sight that they are given by the Holy Spirit for the benefit of the church. The purpose of spiritual gifts is for serving others, or as Paul has said, for the edification of the church rather than enhancing the reputation and glory of those who possess them. The common good of the congregation should never be sacrificed in the interest of personal glory. Liberty in the Spirit and the use of spiritual gifts must be governed by responsibility to the community of believers. As the death and resurrection of Christ were for others, our use of spiritual gifts should be for others, too (1 Corinthians 12:7; 14:26; Philippians 2:3-4).

Love and gifts of the Spirit. A good way to understand the *gifts* and *fruit* of the Holy Spirit is to explore the relationship between the two. Paul in his instructions to the church in Corinth, told them that *love* (the crowning fruit of the Spirit), was to be active and central in their desire for and use of spiritual gifts (1 Corinthians 12:31; 13:1-3, 13; 14:1).

Observe in 12:31 how Paul couples together *the gifts* and *the fruit*. The apostle speaks of the "*more excellent way*," which is the fruit of the Spirit, especially love, regulating the use of the gifts. When the gifts are used in the foremost fruit of the Spirit—*love*, the church is strengthened spiritually or numerically, or both. This is the *more excellent way.*

Similarities and differences between *fruit of the Spirit* and *gifts of the Spirit*. To consider the relationship between the fruit and the gifts, note the following:

Similarities:

- Both the *fruit* and the *gifts* have their origin in the Holy Spirit. *Spiritual gifts* are given by the Holy Spirit for particular Christian service or ministry. The Spirit puts forth *spiritual fruit* as a foundation for living the Christian life in Jesus Christ.

- The purpose of both the fruit and the gifts of Spirit is to build up the community of believers. *Gifts of the Spirit* profit the church (1 Corinthians 12:7; 14:26) and likewise *love, the first fruit of the Spirit,* builds up others (8:1).

- The full and mature expression of the *fruit* and the *gifts* of the Spirit is brought about through Christian growth and maturity. In the Corinthian church, the problem was not a deficiency of spiritual gifts (1:7), but a lack of maturity in the use of the gifts. The *fruit of Love* regulating the *gifts* would have brought about their mature and proper expression in the church.

Differences:

- A Christian should live in and reflect all the *fruit of the Spirit,* but God does not require a Christian to have all the *gifts of the Spirit.* The Holy Spirit is in control of the distribution of the gifts (12:11), and He bestows them on individual believers so that there is a balance of ministry in the church. Each one of us should earnestly desire and be receptive to the spiritual gifts that God wants to give us (12:31; 14:26).

- The *fruit of the Spirit* are devotional and ethical. They produce the likeness of Christ in us. Whereas the *gifts of the Spirit* are charismatic, enabling us to serve others and to do ministry.

- While *gifts of the Spirit* have a vital place in the ministry of the church until the kingdom of God fully comes, the *fruit of the Spirit* are eternal. Gifts of the Spirit such as prophecy, tongues, and knowledge will cease when the kingdom comes in its great power and glory (13:8-10), but faith, hope, and love will continue to abide (v. 13).

The fruit and the gifts of Spirit go hand in hand and work together. They are the work of the Spirit, and both are vital to the Christian life.

—Be—

Spiritual gifts and spiritual maturity. Normally, gifts of the Spirit are manifested through holy people (people whose lives are dedicated to serving God); but as Paul recognizes, the possession of a spiritual gift does not necessarily mean that one has the fruit of the Spirit and is spiritually mature. Paul states: "If I have the gift of prophecy and can fathom all mysteries and all knowledge, and if I have a faith that can move mountains, but do not have love, I am nothing" (1 Corinthians 13:2, NIV). An amazing thing about the Corinthian church is that it did not lack any of the spiritual gifts (1:7). Yet the church was plagued with problems: sexual immorality, lawsuits, and heretical teachings. Even so, Paul affirmed that all the spiritual gifts did indeed exist in the church in Corinth. However, the people in the church were immature in understanding and using them.

As people of God, we want to mature and grow in our faith and our ability to sense the Holy Spirit's guidance, so that we can best use the gifts He gives us to encourage others.

The holiness of spiritual gifts. There is no denying that spiritual gifts are holy—for they come from the Holy Spirit. It is urgent for Spirit-filled believers be holy. Holy people, that is, people who focus their lives on God and live in God's ways, can use their spiritual gifts more effectively. When there is a lack of fruit of the Spirit, a lack of holiness, or a lack dedication on the part of those through whom the gifts are manifested, this hinders and diminishes the positive influence of the spiritual gifts. On the contrary, gifts working through holy vessels strengthens the church spiritually and numerically.

Holy living has eternal dimensions. A life lived in God's holiness is one full of the *fruit of the Spirit*, which assures that the operation of any *gift* that the Holy Spirit may give us will not be hindered or diminished—but will build up the body of Christ. Living holy is very important to the full operation of spiritual gifts in our lives and in the life of the church.

Consider:

- What spiritual gift(s) do you have?

- How would you like to grow and mature in your use of your spiritual gift(s)?

- Can you think of ways that you might express the fruit of *love* through that gift?

—Do—

The Word of God and the *fruit of the Spirit,* especially love, regulate the use of *spiritual gifts.* It is important to follow the teaching of Scripture on the gifts. Otherwise they are very likely to be abused.

Becoming open to gifts of the Spirit. What can we do to open ourselves to being used by the Holy Spirit during our times of worship and fellowship, and avoid manipulating or distorting the gifts? Following are some ideas:

- *We can remember that spiritual gifts are entrusted to followers of Christ by the Holy Spirit.* Since the Holy Spirit has sovereign control of their distribution, the gifts should likewise be manifested under His direction and control. Indeed, spiritual gifts are sacred trusts and are to be used only for the building up of others and the church.

- *We can use spiritual gifts for the benefit of others, being careful to avoid using them in the interest of our own personal glory.*

- *We can allow for freedom in worship, so that within good order there is opportunity for God to interact with us through gifts of the Spirit.* Spiritual gifts manifest God's immediate and concrete presence to heal the brokenhearted, the wounded in soul, those who are afflicted in their bodies, and those who are experiencing other difficulties. Where there is proper order and freedom in worship, people who have gathered to worship will leave their time together blessed.

- *When we encounter people who have gifts of the Spirit, but lack spiritual maturity, we can be gracious and kind and encourage them in the best use of their gifts.* The Corinthians used spiritual gifts, but without understanding the importance of love in their use. Likewise, Balaam and Caiaphas gave prophecies without the fruit of the Spirit (Numbers 22-25; John 11:49-51). Spiritual gifts are more useful to God and the church if they are manifested in humility and love.

- *We can invite the Holy Spirit into our worship.* To allow the Spirit's gifts to operate through our worship and fellowship with each other, we need to welcome the Holy Spirit with open hearts—and avoid quenching or grieving the Holy Spirit (Ephesians 4:30; 1 Thessalonians 5:19). The spontaneous oral gifts have their place in public worship, along with good flexible order, and sound teaching (1 Corinthians 14:12-19).

Consider:

- What is your experience with gifts of the Holy Spirit being manifested in worship?

- How have you been blessed by their use?

- Have you ever observed any problems due to lack of order or maybe the absence of gifts in worship? If so, what have you prayed or done during those times?

The *fruit of the Spirit* and *gifts of the Spirit* always complement each other and never compete. They are a perfect pair, working together to the glory of Jesus Christ and to the building up of the church and people.

Offer a Prayer

Holy Spirit, thank You for Your blessings of spiritual fruit and gifts. I pray that You will grow all Your fruit in me, and will show me the gifts You have given me. Teach me and guide me in using my spiritual gifts. Help me show the love of Jesus in all that I do. Amen.

Day 5

The Spirit and the Modern Pentecostal Movement

Searching the Scripture

Read Acts 2:32-33, 38-39 and Ephesians 4:1-3.

Acts 2:32-33, 38-39:

> This Jesus God has raised up, of which we are all witnesses. Therefore being exalted to the right hand of God, and having received from the Father the promise of the Holy Spirit, He poured out this which you now see and hear . . . Then Peter said to them, "Repent, and let every one of you be baptized in the name of Jesus Christ for the remission of sins; and you shall receive the gift of the Holy Spirit. For the promise is to you and to your children, and to all who are afar off, as many as the Lord our God will call."

Ephesians 4:1-3:

> Walk worthy of the calling with which you were called, with all lowliness and gentleness, with longsuffering, bearing with one another in love, endeavoring to keep the unity of the Spirit in the bond of peace.

Answer the Following Questions:

1. Why do you think the Pentecostal Movement has grown as it has?

2. How would you describe the Pentecostal revival that has flourished in many countries?

3. Can you identify and explain briefly the biblical doctrines that Pentecostals emphasize? (Acts 2:32-33).

4. As followers of Christ, as we walk through life in the presence and empowerment of the Holy Spirit, how do you think we should live? (Ephesians 4:1-3; Galatians 5:22-25)

Yielding to the Spirit

—*Know*—

Pentecostals—people of the Word and the Spirit. In the reading of the Bible, it is clear that God intended for Christianity to be Pentecostal, for all followers of Christ to be led and empowered by the Holy Spirit (Joel 2:28-31; Luke 24:49; Acts 1:8; 2:1-4, 16-21, 33, 38-39; 9:17-19; 10:44-46; 19:1-7). In much of the time from the first century to Azusa Street in Los Angeles, California, in 1906, there have been pockets of Pentecostals here and there in the world. But the outpouring of the Holy Spirit on Azusa Street has marked the beginning of the modern Pentecostal Movement for most Pentecostals. Because this movement has been rooted in God's Word and the Holy Spirit, Pentecostals have come to be known as *people of the Word and the Spirit.*

A brief look at the history of the church. As we look at Christianity from a historical point of view, we can identify three major branches of the Christian church—Roman Catholic, Protestant, and Pentecostal. In light of the accounts in the New Testament, the early church was Pentecostal.

Later, as the Christian church evolved, it became more structured. The existence of organizational structures, creeds, and institutional leadership that have developed in Christianity are not unchristian or anti-Christian in themselves, for they can be very helpful in the life of the church. (For example, they can encourage unity, communicate beliefs, help people grow in faith, and help the church to engage in ministry.) However, some of the structures, rules, and practices that were established over time, have not been in keeping with the teachings of Jesus and the practices of the very early church of the New Testament.

Early Catholicism. Out of an over-emphasis on organization, by the end of the first century, there began to emerge highly organized, hierarchical structures. One of these structured church institutions became known as the Roman Catholic Church. At that time, the manner in which the Catholic Church's leadership was leading the church was not in keeping with the love and grace of Jesus, and their actions quenched the Spirit. The apostle Paul had warned the earlier Christians of this danger (1 Thessalonians 5:19).

Protestant Reformation. In the sixteenth century, the Protestant Reformers discovered that the practices and doctrine of the Roman Catholic Church had stifled the message of the apostles of the New Testament. The Reformers proclaimed, *"justification by faith"* and the *priesthood of all believers.*

Modern Pentecostalism. Then, as we have already noted, the modern-day Pentecostal Movement began early in the twentieth century with a strong emphasis on the baptism in the Holy Spirit and evangelism. The modern movement is understood to have begun in North America in 1901 with Charles Fox Parham's Bible College (Methodist) in Topeka, Kansas. A group of students at the college studied the Book of Acts and concluded that speaking in tongues was the undeniable sign of being baptized in the Spirit.

From that Bible College, the Pentecostal message began to spread over the Midwest, until it reached the Azusa Street Mission in 1906. There the Holy Spirit was poured out similarly to the first Christian Pentecost in Acts 2. A revival (1906–09) started under the leadership of an African-American, William Seymour. This revival movement spread rapidly to many parts of the earth. The focus of the movement was on salvation, baptism in the Spirit after conversion, spiritual gifts, evangelism, and the second coming.

Recently, this movement has been called *"the third force"* of Christianity because of its extraordinary growth, and the fact that it follows the movements of Roman Catholicism and Protestantism. It has been estimated that Pentecostals number 500–750 million in the world today. Indeed, the Pentecostal Movement has become a global movement.

—*Be*—

There are many doctrinal crosscurrents in the church. Today, Pentecostals in the congregation and in the pulpit need to be people who can discern doctrinal truth and error. From the beginning of the modern Pentecostal revival, the Bible has governed all belief, experience, and practice. The Pentecostal Movement has been blessed with many leaders who have been committed to examining teachings, manifestations, and conduct on the basis of the Bible. It is imperative that we build our churches around the Bible, the guidance of the Holy Spirit, and wise pastoral leadership. The Bible must be our overarching authority for faith and practice, not strong personalities.

Consider:

- How do you think that a person can participate in and be a part of the institutional church, with all its strengths and weaknesses, and remain balanced and grounded in Biblical truth?

- Where do you go for spiritual guidance and encouragement?

—Do—

We must continue to affirm the inherent authority of the Bible. The statements of faith of Pentecostal denominations should be honored also, but their content and authority must be rooted in the Bible. Our view of the Bible is that it states the truth exactly as the Holy Spirit wishes to convey it. Any doctrinal claims are to be consistent with teaching of Scripture.

Consider:

- Might there be specific ways that your church fellowship could grow in their experience with God's Word, so that God (Father, Son, Holy Spirit) remains the focus of everything?

- What kind of outcomes would you expect from such spiritual growth and focus?

Offer a Prayer

Jesus, You came to us as the Word of God in human form, and You built Your church. I thank You for the Christians who have gone before us, who have passed along great wisdom and insights from Your Word. I pray that today through the Holy Spirit, You will give the Pentecostal church and all churches an abiding love for God's Holy Scriptures—that we may learn of You and walk with You all the days of our lives. Amen.

Group Discussion

Key Scripture—Luke 4:18-19

> "The Spirit of the Lord is upon Me, because He has anointed Me to preach the gospel to the poor; He has sent Me to heal the brokenhearted, to proclaim liberty to the captives and recovery of sight to the blind, to set at liberty those who are oppressed; To proclaim the acceptable year of the Lord" (Luke 4:18-19).

Opening—This is a time of fellowship and sharing about one another's lives.

Prayer

Testimony—Have two or three group members give a testimony of how God is at work in their lives, whether it is through their daily encounters in this study, or some other way.

Discussion Questions:

1. The Book of Acts indicates that some were filled with the Spirit when hands were placed on them, but others received the fullness of the Spirit without the laying on of hands. How can we explain that?

2. Why is it that speaking in tongues in public worship is to be followed by the gift of interpretation?

3. Explain the relation between the baptism in the Spirit and "the last days" of time.

4. What are some similarities and differences between fruit of the Spirit and gifts of the Spirit@ How do they complement each other in the worship and life of a Spirit-led church?

5. Summarize the history of the modern Pentecostal Movement.

6. Why do you think that the modern Pentecostal Movement has been called "a third force" in Christianity?

7. In this week's study about *The Holy Spirit in the Life of the Church*, what has impacted you the most?

8. What thoughts do you have about what you have learned during these past four weeks?

Closing Prayer

APPENDIX

Spiritual Purposes of Speaking in Tongues (*Glossolalia*) 1 Corinthians, chapters 12, 13, and 14	
Please note: Where the Scripture quotation applies equally to both categories, it extends across both columns.	
Personal Edification	**Edification of the Church**
Definition of *Spiritual edification*: encouragement, confirmation, awakening, blessing of the Holy Spirit	
"He who speaks in a tongue edifies himself" (14:4).	"But the manifestation of the Spirit is given to each one for the profit of all [for the common good]" (12:7).
	"And God has appointed these in the church: first apostles, second prophets, third teachers, after that miracles, then gifts of healings, helps, administrations, varieties of tongues." (12:28).
	"…Do all speak with tongues? Do all interpret?" (12:30).
"Though I speak with the tongues of men and of angels, but have not love, I have become sounding brass or a clanging cymbal" (13:1).	
"Love never fails. But whether there are prophecies, they will fail [come to an end, cease]; whether there are tongues, they will cease…" (13:8).	
"For he who speaks in a tongue does not speak to men but to God, for no one understands him; however, in the spirit he speaks mysteries" (14:2).	
"He who speaks in a tongue edifies himself" (14:4).	
"I wish you all spoke with tongues…" (14:5).	
	"…for he who prophesies is greater than he who speaks with tongues, unless indeed he interprets, that the church may receive edification" (15:5).

"But now, brethren, if I come to you speaking with tongues, what shall I profit you unless I speak to you either by revelation, by knowledge, by prophesying, or by teaching?" (14:6).	
"…unless you utter by the tongue words easy to understand, how will it be known what is spoken? …" (14:9).	
	"Therefore let him who speaks in a tongue pray that he may interpret" (14:13).
"For if I pray in a tongue, my spirit prays, but my understanding is unfruitful" (14:14).	
"…I will pray with the spirit, and I will also pray with the understanding. I will sing with the spirit, and I will also sing with the understanding" (14:15).	
"Otherwise, if you bless with the spirit, how will he who occupies the place of the uninformed say "Amen" at your giving of thanks, since he does not understand what you say? For you indeed give thanks well, but the other is not edified" (14:16, 17).	
"I thank my God I speak with tongues more than you all; yet in the church I would rather speak five words with my understanding, that I may teach others also, than ten thousand words in a tongue" (14:18, 19).	
"Therefore tongues are for a sign, not to those who believe but to unbelievers…" (14:22).	
"Therefore if the whole church comes together in one place, and all speak with tongues, and there come in those who are uninformed or unbelievers, will they not say that you are out of your mind?" (14:23).	

"How is it then, brethren? Whenever you come together, each of you has a psalm, has a teaching, has a tongue, has a revelation, has an interpretation. Let all things be done for edification" (14:26).	
	"If anyone speaks in a tongue, let there be two or at the most three, each in turn, and let one interpret" (14:27).
"But if there is no interpreter, let him keep silent in church, and let him speak to himself and to God" (14:28).	
	"Therefore, brethren, desire earnestly to prophesy, and do not forbid to speak with tongues. Let all things be done decently and in order" (14:39, 40).

* Adapted from: MacDonald, William G. "Distinctions in the Purpose of Glossolalia in 1 Corinthians 12, 13, 14," *Glossolalia in the New Testament.* Springfield, Missouri: Gospel Publishing House, 1964, p. 12-13.

CHURCH OF GOD
DECLARATION OF FAITH

We Believe:

1. In the verbal inspiration of the Bible.
2. In one God eternally existing in three persons; namely, the Father, Son, and Holy Ghost.
3. That Jesus Christ is the only begotten Son of the Father, conceived of the Holy Ghost, and born of the Virgin Mary. That Jesus was crucified, buried, and raised from the dead. That He ascended to heaven and is today at the right hand of the Father as the Intercessor.
4. That all have sinned and come short of the glory of God and that repentance is commanded of God for all and necessary for forgiveness of sins.
5. That justification, regeneration, and the new birth are wrought by faith in the blood of Jesus Christ.
6. In sanctification subsequent to the new birth, through faith in the blood of Christ; through the Word, and by the Holy Ghost.
7. Holiness to be God's standard of living for His people.

8. In the baptism with the Holy Ghost subsequent to a clean heart.

9. In speaking with other tongues as the Spirit gives utterance and that it is the initial evidence of the baptism of the Holy Ghost.

10. In water baptism by immersion, and all who repent should be baptized in the name of the Father, and of the Son, and of the Holy Ghost.

11. Divine healing is provided for all in the atonement.

12. In the Lord's Supper and washing of the saints' feet.

13. In the premillennial second coming of Jesus. First, to resurrect the righteous dead and to catch away the living saints to Him in the air. Second, to reign on the earth a thousand years.

14. In the bodily resurrection; eternal life for the righteous, and eternal punishment for the wicked.

RESOURCES

Books and Articles

Arrington, French L. *Christian Doctrine: A Pentecostal Perspective,* vol. 3, Cleveland, TN: Pathway Press, 1994.

_____, *Encountering the Holy Spirit: Paths of Christian Growth and Service,* Cleveland, TN: Pathway Press, 2003.

_____, *The Greatest Letter Ever Written: A Study of the Book of Romans,* Cleveland, TN: Pathway Press, 2012.

Buffum, Herbert E., lyrics; Dock M. Shanks, music. *He Abides,* 1922.

Evangelical Dictionary of Theology. Grand Rapids, MI: Baker Academic, 2017.

Fire Bible. (Former titles: *Full Life Study Bible* and *Life in the Spirit Study Bible*). Available in: ESV, KJV, and NIV 1984 (Hendrickson Publishers), MEV (Life Publishers, Passion Faith). Also available in other languages from 4THE WORLD Resource Distributors–www.4wrd.org.

Johns, Cheryl Bridges, "Sacred Space" in *Evangelical Dictionary of Theology*. Grand Rapids, MI: Baker Academic, 2017.

Martin, Lee Roy. *Spirit-Filled Worship*, Miami, FL: Senda de Vida Publishers, 2017.

Wiles, J. Ben. *People of the Spirit*, Cleveland: TN, Church of God Adult Discipleship, 2015.

Witt, R. Keith and French L. Arrington, eds. *Issues in Contemporary Pentecostalism*, Cleveland: TN, Pathway Press, 2012.

Websites

BibleGateway.com www.biblegateway.com
Offers various Bible versions and study tools.

BibleStudyTools.com www.biblestudytools.com
Offers various Bible versions and study tools, including an interlinear Bible for word study (English, Hebrew, and Greek). This interlinear Bible is linked to explanation about individual words in the Biblical text. To access, look up a passage in either King James Version or New American Standard Bible, then select the "Interlinear" option.

Church of God (Cleveland, TN)—official website
www.churchofgod.org